Theme Units Kids Adore:
from Ants to Zoos
Grades K-3

Beth Alley Wise

Troll Associates

Interior Illustrations by: Marilyn Barr

ISBN: 0-8167-2586-1

Printed in the United States of America.

10 9 8 7 6 5 4 3 2 1

CONTENTS

INTRODUCTION

This book is filled with easy-to-do activities relating to topics that are among children's favorites.

Each theme in this book contains a collection of activities from a variety of curriculum areas, including language arts, math, science, social studies, art, and music. Suggestions and patterns for learning centers are provided as additional opportunities for fun and hands-on learning.

Each unit in *Theme Units Kids Adore: From Ants to Zoos* begins with a variety of activities carefully designed to provide opportunities for children to learn as a whole class, individually, and in small groups. Each unit contains suggestions for using a theme-related pattern. You may wish to use the pattern as suggested on the page, or you may want to use it as a starting point for content-area learning centers.

ANTS

the jar and have the class observe the ants. Did the ants dig an underground nest? Are there passageways throughout the nest? Are there "rooms" off the tunnels?

Ants on a Log

Slice cleaned celery into 3-inch (8-cm) pieces. Have children use plastic knives or wooden craft sticks to stuff the celery with peanut butter. Place raisin "ants" on top of the celery before eating.

Ant Trails

Take a nature walk. Look for trails of ants on a sidewalk or near a trash can. Explain that the first ant to find food leaves a scent on the ground so that other ants can find the way. Then, one behind the other, the ants follow the trail to the food. Tell children to watch ants as they follow the scent trail.

Ant Nests

Make a home for some ants. Fill a glass jar within 2 inches (5 cm) of the top with soil. Capture a colony of ants and carefully put them in the jar. Dip a damp cottonball in honey and put it in the jar as food for the ants. Poke tiny holes in the jar lid. Wrap a dark cloth around the sides of the jar. After a few days, unwrap

Ant Colonies

Children will be fascinated to learn about ant colonies. As they observe the ant nest from the previous activity, tell them about the different types of ants in the nest. For example, explain that one ant, the queen, leads the others. Have children examine the nest for the queen and for where she has laid eggs.

Next tell children about the worker ants, whose job it is to find food, take care of the eggs and baby ants, guard the colony against enemies, and protect the queen. Have children find worker ants in the nest.

Children will enjoy drawing pictures to show their discoveries. Have children put the ant colony back where they found it once they finish their observations.

Ant Antics

Read stories about ants. Compare the sizes, shapes, and colors of the ants featured in the stories. After you read the stories, let children share something new they learned about ants.

- *Ants Are Fun* by Mildred Myrick (Harper, 1968)
- *Ant Cities* by Arthur Dorros (Harper, 1987)
- *Who Can't Follow an Ant?* by Michael Pellowski (Troll, 1986)

Ant on an Anthill

Copy the poem on the board and read it aloud. Use the poem as a pattern for new writing. Brainstorm other words that rhyme with *see*. Use the rhyming words to help you write new verses for the poem.

Two little ants	Two little ants
On an anthill see	On an anthill see
One big giant	One [sweet smelling flower]
And the giant's ME!	[And a bumblebee.]

Marching Ants

Sing "The Ants Go Marching." Allow children to act out the ants' actions.

THE ANTS GO MARCHING

The ants go marching one by one, hurrah, hurrah!

The ants go marching one by one, hurrah, hurrah!

When the ants go marching one by one

The little one stops to have some fun.

And they all go marching down in the ground to get out of the rain—

BOOM, BOOM, BOOM!

Additional verses:

Two . . . tie its shoe	Six . . . pick up sticks
Three . . . climb a tree	Seven . . . pick up Kevin
Four . . . shut the door	Eight . . . shut the gate
Five . . . take a dive	Nine . . . check the time
Ten . . . say "THE END!"	

Amazing Ants

Tell children that an ant can carry ten times its own weight. Then ask them which of the following things they think an ant could carry.

raisin	cookie crumb	sandwich
cup of milk	spider	grain of rice
birdseed	fly	grain of sugar

Using the Ant Pattern

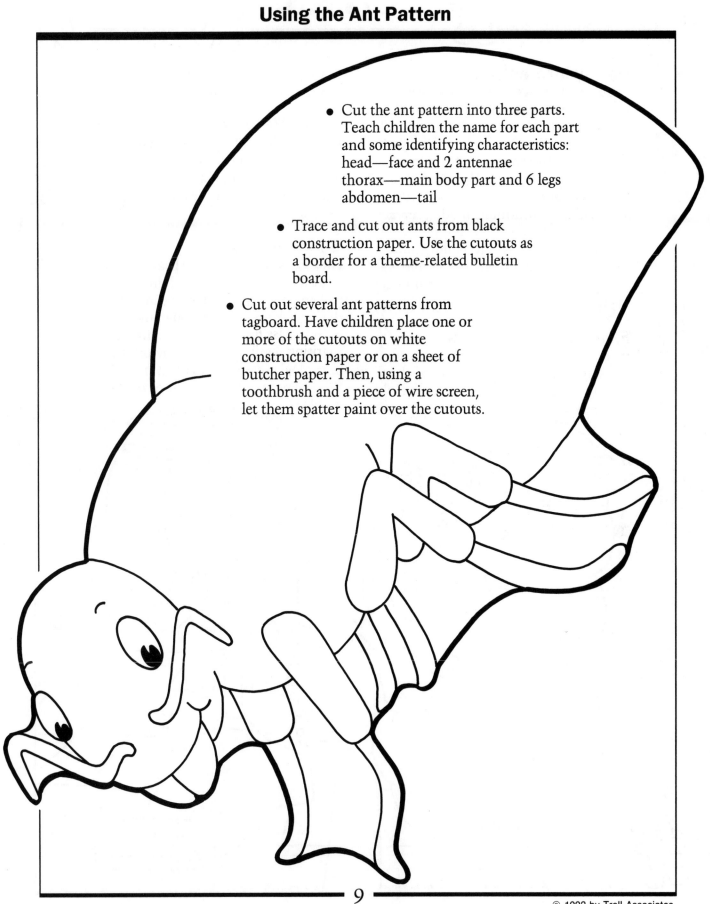

- Cut the ant pattern into three parts. Teach children the name for each part and some identifying characteristics: head—face and 2 antennae thorax—main body part and 6 legs abdomen—tail

- Trace and cut out ants from black construction paper. Use the cutouts as a border for a theme-related bulletin board.

- Cut out several ant patterns from tagboard. Have children place one or more of the cutouts on white construction paper or on a sheet of butcher paper. Then, using a toothbrush and a piece of wire screen, let them spatter paint over the cutouts.

9

BEARS

Bear-y Interesting

Children of all ages love teddy bears. Most children and adults have had at least one teddy bear. But did you know that teddy bears were named for a past president of the United States? On a hunting trip, President Theodore (Teddy) Roosevelt refused to shoot a bear cub that had strayed from its mother. In the newspapers the next day, the president described the cub as soft, cuddly, and cute. At once, toymakers began making stuffed versions of the animal and named them "teddy bears."

Favorite Teddy Bears

Have children bring their favorite teddy bears (or other stuffed animals) to school. During the day, allow time for each child to share his or her bear. Let them talk about it and pass it around.

Teddy Bear Picnic

Read *Teddy Bear's Picnic.* Then place tablecloths, picnic baskets, and paper plates on the floor. Have a real or imaginary picnic for the children and their teddy bears.

Bears In a Jar

Fill a glass jar with plastic bears or bear-shaped cookies. After the children have had an opportunity to look carefully at the jar, ask them to estimate how many bears are inside. Record the estimates on a chart. Then let volunteers count the bears. Did anyone guess the number? Who came the closest to the correct number?

Bear Books

Read stories about Winnie-the-Pooh, Paddington, the Berenstains, and other bears with the children. Or tell a favorite bear story, such as "The Three Bears." After each story, provide bear cutouts for the children to write (or dictate) their favorite parts. Post the cutouts in sequential order. Refer to the cutouts when retelling the stories.

Young readers will love these bear books, too!

- *Bears* by Susan Kuchalla (Troll, 1982)
- *Benny's Bad Day* by Michael Pellowski (Troll, 1986)
- *Brown Bear, Brown Bear, What Do You See?* by Bill Martin, Jr. (Holt, 1983)
- *Corduroy* by Don Freeman (Viking, 1968)
- *Ira Sleeps Over* by Bernard Waber (Houghton Mifflin, 1973)

Bear-ly the Same

Have volunteers retell the story of "The Three Bears." Recall words that Goldilocks used when describing the porridge, the chairs, and the beds. Write the words on the board. Brainstorm other objects that fit into each group.

Hot	Cold	Hard	Soft
sun	ice cube	rock	cotton
oven	ice cream	wood	puppy

hard	soft
rock	cotton
wood	puppy

hot	cold
sun	ice cube
oven	ice cream

Using the Bear Pattern

- Write daily journals on bear cutouts.

- Invite children to write a letter to the author of their favorite bear book. Write the letters on bear-shaped paper.

- Write the word *bear* on the top of a bear pattern. Have volunteers add other words that rhyme with *bear*. Make the list as long as you can.

- Trace and cut out tagboard bears. Let children "paint" watered-down glue over the entire bear. Then sprinkle glitter on top. (Let dry thoroughly before moving.)

Bear Rhyme

Chant the following bear rhyme with children. Create additional rhyming verses. Then have volunteers use teddy bears to act out the movements. Older children may wish to chant the rhyme as they jump rope.

TEDDY BEAR, TEDDY BEAR
Teddy bear, teddy bear, turn around.
Teddy bear, teddy bear, touch the ground.
Teddy bear, teddy bear, reach up high.
Teddy bear, teddy bear, touch the sky.
Teddy bear, teddy bear, arms out wide.
Teddy bear, teddy bear, touch your side.
Teddy bear, teddy bear, touch your shoe.
Teddy bear, teddy bear, I love you!

Real Bears

Collect pictures of real bears in their natural surroundings and display them in the science center. Talk about real bears. Have children help you list some facts about each bear.

THE BEAR FACTS
Bears are mammals.
Cubs drink milk from
their mother's body.
Most bears sleep all winter.
Compared to humans,
most bears are big.

Bear Walk

Invite children to walk like bears. On all fours, have them move their right hand and left leg at the same time, then their left hand and right leg.

BUGS

Big Beehive, Little Beehive

Create a "buggy" atmosphere in your room. Staple cardboard egg cartons to a bulletin board to simulate a beehive. Have children paint and cut out bees to put in, on, and around the beehive. Tell children to make one bee, the queen, larger than the others, making sure she is inside the hive and guarded by some worker bees.

Let children make beehive pencil holders for their desks. Have them glue four egg carton cups together (three on the bottom, one centered on top), paint or cut an opening in the hive (the middle cup), and then paint bees on the hive. As a last step, tell children to poke a hole in the top of the hive for a pencil.

Busy as a Bee

After asking children what they think the saying "busy as a bee" means, record the responses on a chart. Invite them to illustrate the chart.

Beekeeper

Invite a beekeeper to your class to tell about the job. Ask the beekeeper to bring some equipment used to raise bees. If possible, ask the beekeeper to bring in a working hive. (Be sure to keep the bees in a place away from the children!)

A Bunch of Bees

Display pictures of bumblebees. Help children count the number of wings, legs, and antennae each bee has. Make a chart to record the numbers.

Bees	
antennae	2
wings	4
legs	6

Baby Bumblebees

Make thumbprint bees. Have children press their thumbs onto a black ink pad and then onto an index card. Use a felt-tip pen to help children draw features for the baby bumblebees.

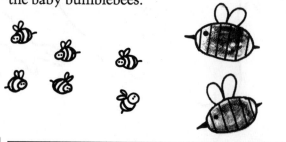

Ladybug, Ladybug, Fly Away Home!

Recite the nursery rhyme as children pretend to be ladybugs flying home.

Ladybug! Ladybug! Fly away home.
Your house is on fire.
Your children have gone,
All but one, and her name is Ann,
She hid under a frying pan.

Ladybug Look-alikes

Gather a bucket of smooth rocks. Let each child pick a rock and describe it to the class. Encourage them to use words such as *smooth, round, flat, bumpy,* and *hard.* Provide red and black tempera and paintbrushes for the children to paint the rocks to look like ladybugs.

An Unladylike Ladybug

Share Eric Carle's book, *The Grouchy Ladybug,* with children. Then invite interested children to make a stick puppet for each character in the story. Use the puppets to retell the story.

Ladybug Lineup

Precut ten ladybug patterns. Write a numeral from 1–10 on the head of each ladybug. Have children put the ladybugs in numerical order on a table. Then have them place the corresponding number of paper circles (colored counters or buttons work well, too) on each ladybug.

Legs on a Ladybug

Have children observe a ladybug under a magnifying glass. Tell them to count the number of legs on the ladybug and compare it to the number of legs on the bumblebee. Does the ladybug have more legs? Fewer legs? Or the same number of legs? Ask children to count the number of wings and antennae on the ladybug. Have them tell how these numbers compare to the bee. Record the numbers.

Graceful Grasshoppers

Have children imitate the movement of a grasshopper as it hops. Point out that grasshoppers have powerful hind legs that enable them to jump long distances with little effort.

Clay Grasshoppers

Shape a grasshopper body from clay. Bend pieces of pipe cleaners to form wings, legs, and antennae. Press the wings, legs, and antennae into the body.

Grasshopper Hotel

Cut two windows in an empty oatmeal box. Tape nylon netting inside the box to cover the windows. Take a walk around the school or in a nearby park to look for grasshoppers. Find two or three and put them inside the grasshopper "hotel." Keep the lid on the box while the grasshoppers are visiting. Provide a magnifying glass for a close-up look at the grasshoppers. Have children count the number of legs on each grasshopper. Ask them how this number compares with the number of legs found on a bee or on a ladybug. Let children look for other similarities in the bugs: number of wings, body parts, joints in legs, antennae, and so on. Release the grasshoppers when finished.

Sing a Song of Grasshoppers

Sing to the tune of "Battle Hymn of the Republic."

GRASSHOPPER

The first grasshopper jumped right over the
    second grasshopper's back,
Oh, the first grasshopper jumped right over
    the second grasshopper's back,
The first grasshopper jumped right over the
    second grasshopper's back,
Oh, the first grasshopper jumped right over.
They were only playing leapfrog.
They were only playing leapfrog,
They were only playing leapfrog,
When the first grasshopper jumped right over.

Using the Bug Patterns

- Have children write books about bugs. Make covers and pages for the books shaped like bees, ladybugs, or grasshoppers.

Trace the patterns onto poster board. Punch holes around the edges and let children use a bobby pin and yarn to sew the outline of each bug.

Cut out several bees, ladybugs, and grasshoppers from felt. Place the shapes on flannelboard. Let children create addition or subtraction stories that involve the bugs.

Cut out one set of bugs. On the bee, list words that begin with *b*. On the ladybug, list words that begin with *l*. On the grasshopper, list words that begin with *gr*.

BUNNIES

Bunny Buddies

Encourage children to bring stuffed bunnies from home. Let them share their bunnies with the class, telling the bunny's name and something special about it. Allow bunnies to join the class during rest time, story time, and other quiet times. (Collect extra stuffed bunnies to be sure that every child has a bunny buddy.)

Bunny Finger Play

Share the finger play with children. Then ask them to perform the motions as you chant the rhyme together.

Here is a bunny with ears so funny,
(Hold up index and middle fingers, wiggle them.)

And here is his hole in the ground.
(Make hole with other hand.)

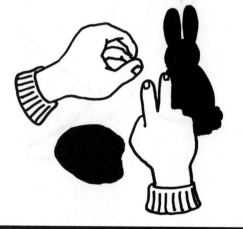

When a noise he hears, he pricks his ears
(Hold index and middle fingers up straight.)

And he hops in his hole in the ground.
("Rabbit" jumps into hole made by other hand.)

Pet Bunnies

Invite a local pet shop owner to bring a real bunny to your class. Encourage the owner to explain how to care for the pet, including handling, grooming, feeding, and exercise.

How Many Is a "Bunch" of Bunnies?

Read the book *Bunches and Bunches of Bunnies* by Louise Mathews. As you reread the book, think up math problems for the pages. For example, two bunnies are eating cabbage and three bunnies are eating carrots. How many bunnies are there in all? Write the addition sentence 2 + 3 = 5.

Write your own version of *Bunches and Bunches of Bunnies.* Prepare a big book with blank pages. On each spread, have children write or dictate a story involving addition with a bunch of bunnies. Have volunteers illustrate each page. Write the addition sentence and the answer on the page, but hide the answer under a paper flap.

Bunny Biscuits

Using canned biscuit dough, provide two biscuits for each child. Instruct children to cut one biscuit in half. Pinch the bunny's ears (biscuit halves) onto the bunny's head (whole biscuit). Use raisins or nuts for the nose and eyes. Use slivered almonds or shredded coconut for whiskers. Bake and eat.

Bigger than a Bunny

Tape a yardstick or meterstick on the wall, with the base against a table. Display bunnies children brought from home. Let children predict how tall each bunny is and record the predictions. Then measure each bunny and record the height. Compare the predictions and the correct measurements.

Bunny Books

Hop on over to the library shelf or reading center and enjoy these books about bunnies!

- *Bunches and Bunches of Bunnies* by Louise Mathews (Putnam, 1978)
- *Busy Bunnies* by Stephen Caitlin (Troll, 1988)
- *The Great Bunny Race* by Kathy Feczko (Troll, 1985)
- *Rabbits Can't Dance!* by Dale Binford (Gareth Stevens, 1989)
- *The Runaway Bunny* by Margaret Brown (Harper, 1972)
- *The Velveteen Rabbit* by Margery Williams (Troll, 1988)
- *What a Funny Bunny* by Patricia Whitehead (Troll, 1985)

Bunny Buns

Make six bunnies. Cut tagboard circles for the head and body. Cut and glue on a different material for each bunny's tail: cotton, sandpaper, fabric, crumpled foil, fur, corrugated cardboard. Put another sample of each material in a "feely" bag or box. Let children use one hand to feel the first bunny's tail and the other hand to find the same material in the "feely bag." Repeat until all children have had a turn.

Bunny Tracks and Bunny Facts

Prepare in advance and hide a stuffed bunny with a card stating a fact about real bunnies. Cut fifteen to twenty bunny footprints from tagboard. Tape the pawprints on the floor leading from a central location to the bunny's hiding place. Let children take turns tracking the bunny and reading the card. Each day, change the hiding place, card, and redirect the tracks to lead to the bunny.

Funny Bunny

Make bunnies from two paper plates. Cut the first plate as shown. Glue the "ears" to the whole plate. Glue on broom straw for whiskers and construction paper or felt for the bunny's eyes, nose, and mouth.

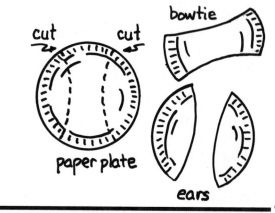

cut   cut

bowtie

paper plate

ears

- Trace and cut out several bunny patterns. Write pairs of antonyms on the bunny ears. Cut one ear off each bunny. Let children complete the bunnies by matching opposites.

- Roll out clay on a flat surface. Place a bunny pattern on top of the clay and use a toothpick to punch holes around the outline. Then pick up the pattern and cut through the outline with a plastic knife or a wooden craft stick.

- Precut several bunnies from construction paper. Paint a woodland scene on a long sheet of butcher paper. Let children find places in the picture that would make good homes for the bunnies. Glue the bunnies in their woodland homes.

BUTTERFLIES

Butterfly on a Glove

Make glove puppets. For each puppet, you will need a garden glove, pom-poms, glue, and scraps of felt. Glue green pom-poms together to make a caterpillar. Glue the caterpillar on the back of the thumb. Use one large pom-pom and felt to make a large, colorful butterfly. Glue the butterfly on the back of the glove. Make an egg, sun, strawberry, leaf, and cocoon to glue on the fingers of the palm-side of the glove. Use the puppet to teach the life cycle of a butterfly.

Bellyache for a Butterfly

Pretend you have a caterpillar cupped in your hands. Talk softly to the caterpillar, as though comforting it: "Do you have a bellyache? Why?" Invite children to tiptoe to the reading area and sit quietly while you solicit suggestions for making the caterpillar feel better.

Tell children that you know another caterpillar that had the same problem. Read *The Very Hungry Caterpillar* by Eric Carle to find out what happened.

Cast of Caterpillars

Encourage volunteers to retell *The Very Hungry Caterpillar* using the glove puppets made earlier.

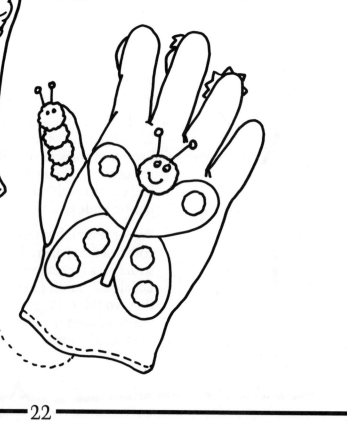

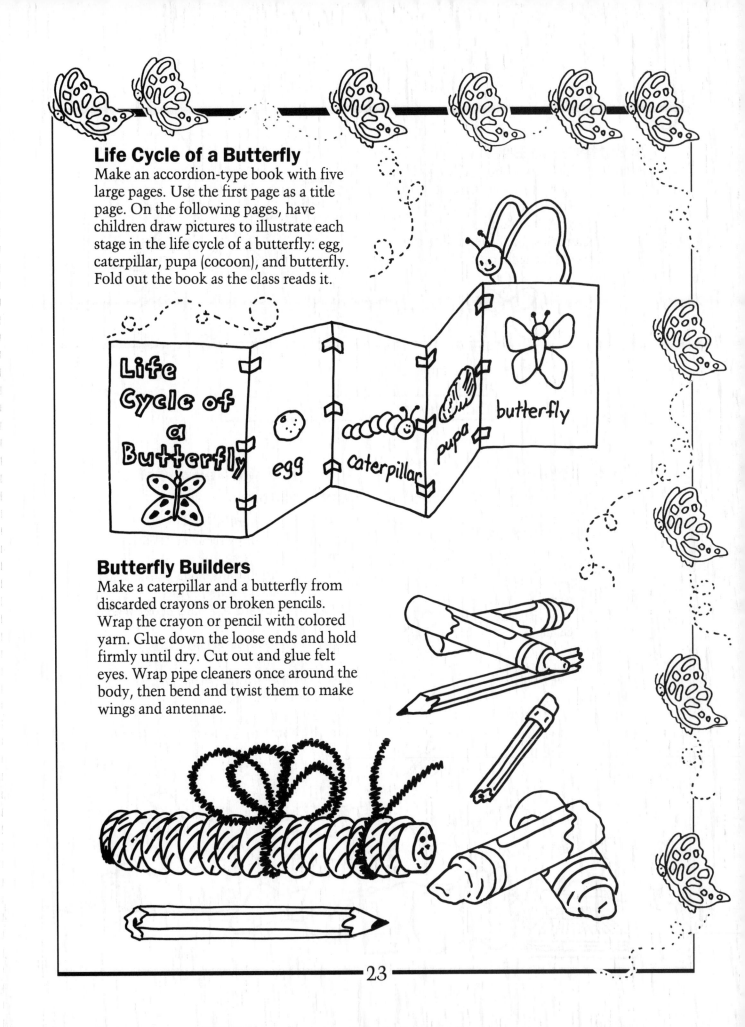

Life Cycle of a Butterfly

Make an accordion-type book with five large pages. Use the first page as a title page. On the following pages, have children draw pictures to illustrate each stage in the life cycle of a butterfly: egg, caterpillar, pupa (cocoon), and butterfly. Fold out the book as the class reads it.

Life Cycle of a Butterfly

egg

caterpillar

pupa

butterfly

Butterfly Builders

Make a caterpillar and a butterfly from discarded crayons or broken pencils. Wrap the crayon or pencil with colored yarn. Glue down the loose ends and hold firmly until dry. Cut out and glue felt eyes. Wrap pipe cleaners once around the body, then bend and twist them to make wings and antennae.

A Butterfly in Brief

Borrow a collection of butterflies and moths from a butterfly enthusiast. Display the insects for children to inspect and compare. Ask children to identify the characteristics that differentiate the two insects. Make a chart to show the differences.

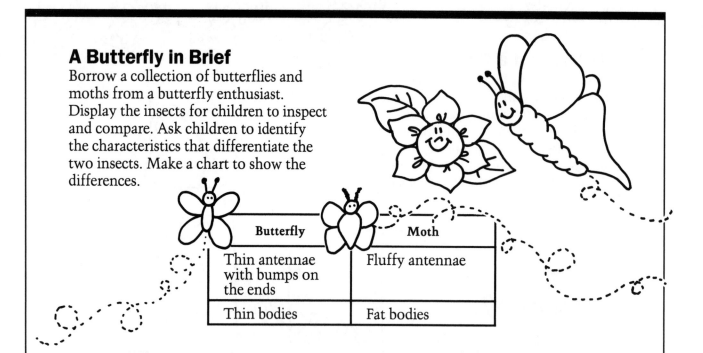

Butterfly	Moth
Thin antennae with bumps on the ends	Fluffy antennae
Thin bodies	Fat bodies

A Pet Butterfly

Sing "Found a Butterfly" to the tune of "Clementine."

FOUND A BUTTERFLY

Found a butterfly,
found a butterfly,
found a yellow butterfly.
It was sipping the sweet nectar
from a flower by the fence.
Tried to catch him
in a bug net,
to keep him for my pet.
But he fluttered by,
oh, sweet butterfly.
Haven't caught a pet yet!

Books to Take You out of Your Cocoon

- *Discovering Butterflies* by Douglas Florian (Macmillan, 1986)
- *From Egg to Butterfly* by Marlene Reidel (Carolrhoda Books, 1981)
- *The Lamb and the Butterfly* by Arnold Sundgard (Orchard Books Watts, 1988)
- *Look, a Butterfly* by David Cutts (Troll, 1982)
- *The Very Hungry Caterpillar* by Eric Carle (Putnam, 1981)
- *Who Will Fly with Butterfly?* by Lorice Hartmann (Valkyrie Publishing, 1978)

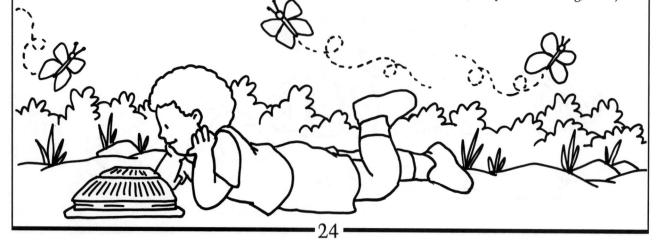

Using the Butterfly Pattern

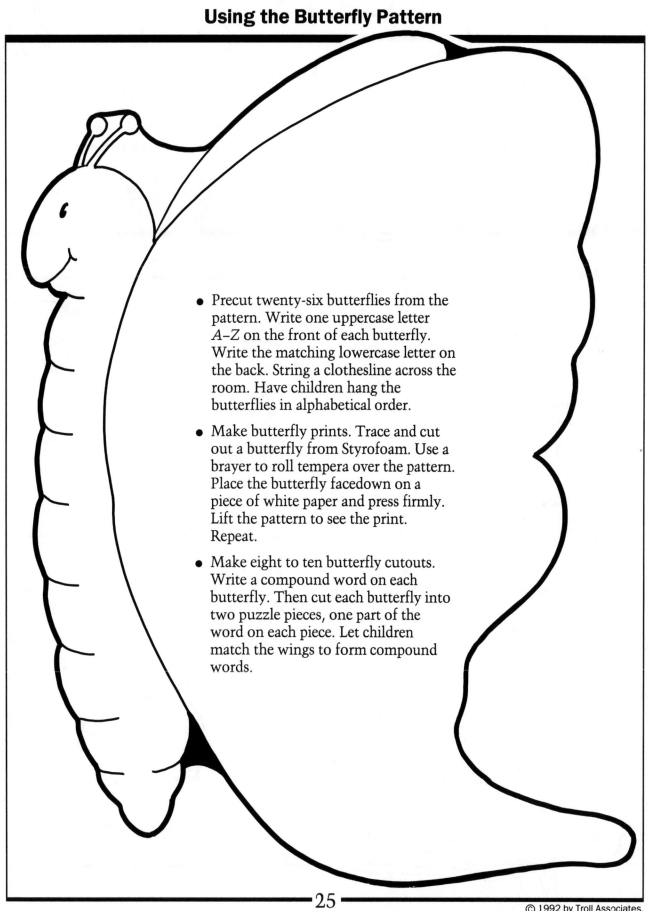

- Precut twenty-six butterflies from the pattern. Write one uppercase letter *A–Z* on the front of each butterfly. Write the matching lowercase letter on the back. String a clothesline across the room. Have children hang the butterflies in alphabetical order.

- Make butterfly prints. Trace and cut out a butterfly from Styrofoam. Use a brayer to roll tempera over the pattern. Place the butterfly facedown on a piece of white paper and press firmly. Lift the pattern to see the print. Repeat.

- Make eight to ten butterfly cutouts. Write a compound word on each butterfly. Then cut each butterfly into two puzzle pieces, one part of the word on each piece. Let children match the wings to form compound words.

CATS

Cat Kisses

Read the poem "Cat Kisses" by Bobbi Katz (from Jack Prelutsky's *Read-Aloud Rhymes for the Very Young*). Don't share the title of the poem or the pictures at first. Let children guess what furry thing gives sandpaper kisses.

Curl up with a Cat

Invite children to bring in from home their favorite books about kittens and cats. Display the books on a reading table or library shelf. Allow plenty of time for children to thumb through the books and to share theirs with a friend.

Some great cat capers to read aloud:
- *Fish for Supper* by Morgan Matthews (Troll, 1986)
- *Hi, Cat!* by Ezra Jack Keats (Macmillan, 1988)
- *The Kid's Cat Book* by Tomie De Paola (Holiday, 1979)
- *Millions of Cats* by Wanda Gag (Putnam, 1977)
- *My Cat Loves to Hide in Boxes* by Eve Sutton (Penguin, 1973)

Pur-r-r-fect Picture

Draw the outline of a cat on a large piece of construction paper. Brush the inside of the cat thinly with glue. Sprinkle sand over the picture. Let dry, then shake off excess sand.

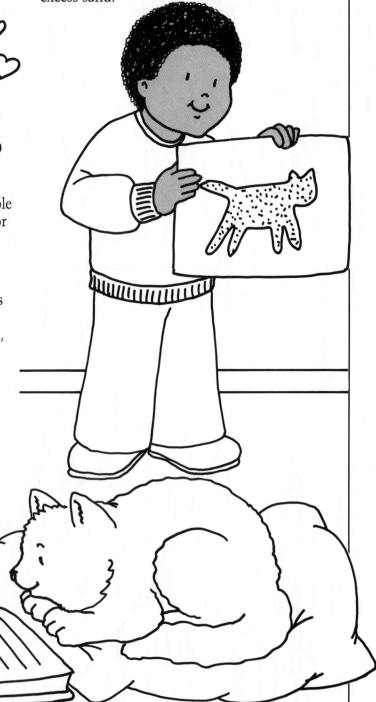

Prize Cat

Have a cat show, inviting children to enter their own cats. Divide the cats into three cat-egories: real, stuffed, other (clay, painted, drawn). As the cats in each group are presented, let the class determine the characteristics that make that cat unique. Take photographs of the cats and hang them on the bulletin board, each with the name of the owner and a list of the cat's special features. Award blue ribbons to all the participants.

Betsy's Cat, Tabby
Soft fur, bright green eyes

Pull-Out Cat Riddles

Draw and cut out a large paper cat. Cut a slit 1 1/2 inches (3 1/4 cm) wide on the cat's mouth. Write a cat riddle on the cutout. Then cut a strip of paper 1 inch (2 1/2 cm) wide. Staple a tab to the right end of the strip. Starting on the left end of the strip, write "Pull" and then the answer to the riddle. Place the answer strip in the slit in the cat's mouth. Children will pull the strip through the slit to reveal the answer. Invite children to read and answer each riddle.

What does a cat have that no other animal has?

Pull. Kittens.

Come, Kitty!

Share the finger play with children. Read it through one time and perform the actions. Then let children join in with you.

Kitten Is Hiding

A kitten is hiding under a chair.
  (Hide one thumb under hand.)
I looked and looked for her everywhere.
  (Turn head from side to side.)
Under the table and under the bed;
  (Pretend to look.)
I looked in the corner, and when I said, "Come, Kitty, come, Kitty, here's milk for you."
  (Cup hands to form dish.)
Kitty came running and calling, "Mew, mew."
  (Hold and pat imaginary kitty.)

Cat Couplets

Help children write two-line rhymes. Encourage them to draw or paint pictures to go with each rhyme. Here are a few to get you started on the right paw.

A silly cat wears a _____.

Two cold kittens Put on their _____.

Cat Myths

On strips of paper write myths or questions about cats. Place the strips in a cat-shaped envelope. Each day, draw one strip from the envelope and read it aloud. Let children try to answer the questions on their own, then, if necessary, provide the correct answer.

QUESTION: Do cats have nine lives?
ANSWER: Cats *seem* to have nine lives because they often escape from dangerous situations. Cats can run and jump so easily, they can get away from trouble much faster than you and I.

QUESTION: Why do cats have whiskers?
ANSWER: Cats have whiskers to use as feelers in the dark. The whiskers help the cat find its way in the dark.

QUESTION: Can you teach a cat new tricks?
ANSWER: Cats love challenges and the attention their owners pay them. So if you spend much time with your cat, you may be able to teach it to roll over, chase a toy, or jump through a hoop. When you play with your cat, always show it love and kindness and don't force it to do a trick.

Mittens for Kittens

Provide three different pairs of mittens and let children match the pairs.

Then read the nursery rhyme "Three Little Kittens" to the children. Let them use the mittens as props for acting out the rhyme.

Compare Cats

Cover a bulletin board with pictures of cats and kittens from magazines, coloring books, and greeting cards. Help children group the cats by color, shape, or size.

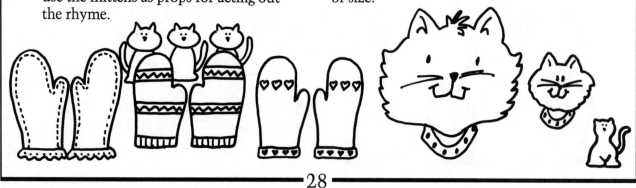

Using the Cat Pattern

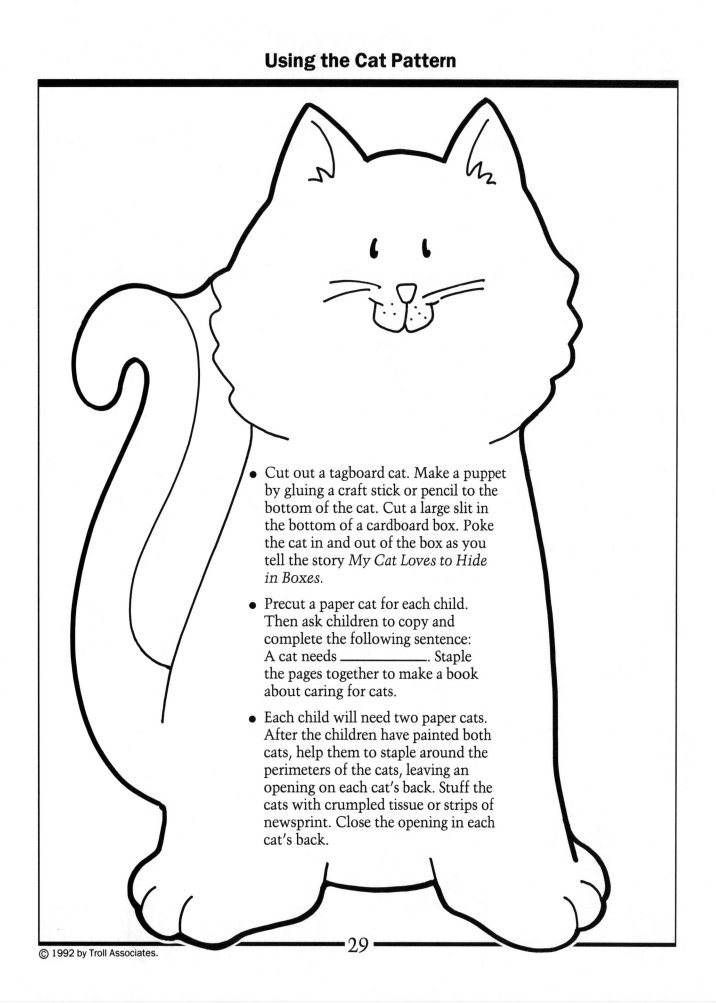

- Cut out a tagboard cat. Make a puppet by gluing a craft stick or pencil to the bottom of the cat. Cut a large slit in the bottom of a cardboard box. Poke the cat in and out of the box as you tell the story *My Cat Loves to Hide in Boxes.*

- Precut a paper cat for each child. Then ask children to copy and complete the following sentence: A cat needs _____. Staple the pages together to make a book about caring for cats.

- Each child will need two paper cats. After the children have painted both cats, help them to staple around the perimeters of the cats, leaving an opening on each cat's back. Stuff the cats with crumpled tissue or strips of newsprint. Close the opening in each cat's back.

Circus Parade

Provide "band" instruments: pots, pans, and spoons; drums; horns; cymbals or pan lids; wood blocks; kazoos; tambourines. Have some children assume the role of circus clowns, playing the instruments as they come into town. Other clowns in the parade may wish to wheel stuffed animals in wheelbarrows or wagons, or do cartwheels or silly tricks as they travel along the parade route.

Clown Around with Numbers

Using a paper plate and construction paper, make a clown face similar to the one shown. Add a tall paper hat. Copy the sets of dots and the numbers onto the hat. Punch a hole under each numeral. Have children poke a pencil through the hole that names the number of dots in each set. Make a circle around the hole on the back side of the hat to mark the correct answer.

Clown Hats

Make clown hats from 18 inch × 24 inch (46 cm × 60 cm) construction paper. Cut a pattern as shown here. Have children trace and cut their own clown hats, then decorate them. Roll each hat to form a cone and staple. Glue crepe paper or strips of tissue to the top.

Clever Clowns

Have children trace their hands on white paper. Decorate the fingers and thumb and the clown's face. Use yarn, pom-poms, felt scraps, and paper to add hair and facial features. Cut and paste a paper hat on top.

Cory Dent

What a funny clown.

Clown Poems

Brainstorm a list of action words that apply to clowns. End each verb with *-ing*. Use the words on the list to create a class poem about clowns. Follow this pattern:

TITLE	Clowns
(2 verbs)	——, ——,
(3 verbs)	——, ——, ——,
(2 verbs)	——, ——,
END	Clowns

Collect Clown Classics

Collect books and poems about clowns for independent reading or read-aloud times. Let children illustrate their favorite clowns from the poems and books.

- *The Clown's Smile* by Mike Thaler (Harper, 1986)
- *The Clown-Arounds Go on Vacation* by Joanna Cole (Parents, 1984)
- *I Want to Be a Clown* by Sharon Johnson (School Zone, 1985)
- *This Is My Trunk* by Steven Harris (Macmillan, 1985)

Clowning Around

Perform the actions to the finger play as you read the words aloud. Then invite children to join you as you repeat the rhyme.

THE CIRCUS CLOWN

The circus clown
(Hands form a cone-shaped hat over head.)
Has a funny face,
(Make silly face.)
With a red, red, nose right HERE.
(Point to own nose.)
Can YOU make a face
(Point to children one by one.)
Like a circus clown,
With a smile from ear to ear?
(Draw up corners of mouth.)

Catch a Clown

Invite a real clown to visit and show children how to dress and to put on makeup. Most clowns "adopt" a name and a personality of their own. Ask the visitor to tell about himself or herself and about what it is like to be a clown.

Have adult volunteers paint clown faces on the children. Let class clowns practice and then present their own circus acts. You may wish to provide props such as buckets, wagons, hats, balloons, and the like. Have a ringmaster introduce each clown.

Clown on a Tightrope

Place a 5-foot (1 1/2-meter) piece of rope along the floor. Let class clowns try their skill at walking the tightrope. Encourage them to walk slowly, with their eyes straight ahead and their arms out to their sides for better balance.

- Have children list circus words on clown cutouts. Encourage them to make the lists as long as possible.

- Have children suggest ways to cheer up a very sad clown. Record the suggestions on clown cutouts. Post the children's suggestions on a bulletin board inside the room or in the hallway outside the room for others to enjoy.

- Trace and cut out clowns. Let children "paint" watered-down glue over the entire clown. Then cover the clown with pieces of torn tissue paper. Use scissors to trim around the edges of the clown cutout.

- Write a class thank-you note to the visiting clown.

Fossil Hunt

Read with children *The Berenstain Bears and the Missing Dinosaur Bone* by Stan and Jan Berenstain or *Digging up Dinosaurs* by Aliki.

Boil chicken bones in a pot of salt water. "Bury" the sterilized bones in a box of sand. Let children take turns digging for the "dinosaur fossils" in the sand.

Fun with Fossils

Help children make discoveries about fossils by seeing how dinosaurs left prints long ago.

Have each child flatten a piece of clay on wax paper until the clay is about 1 inch (2 1/2 cm) thick. Then press a plastic dinosaur into the clay. Remove the dinosaur and have children examine the print.

FOSSIL HUNT

Dinosaur Skeletons

Display books and pictures that show a variety of dinosaurs and their skeletons. Talk about the skeletons, pointing to and naming major bones, teeth, bony plates, spikes, and horns.

Provide large, tagboard dinosaur cutouts. Have children work in pairs to glue the chicken bones on the dinosaur cutouts to make skeletons.

Dinosaur Fact Books

Fold several sheets of paper in half. Staple the pages in the center to create a book. Have children draw a picture of a different dinosaur on each page. Then encourage them to write two or three facts about each dinosaur pictured. Post the books on a bulletin board inside the room or on a wall outside the room for others to enjoy.

Dare You, Dinosaur!

Collect dinosaur books and put them in a large box. Then, from poster board, draw and cut out the head of a triceratops. Cut a large opening for the dinosaur's mouth. Tape the head onto the top of the box. Beware of the dinosaur's bite as you pull books from its mouth!

You may wish to add the following books to your "dangerously good" collection about dinosaurs.

- *Digging up Dinosaurs* by Aliki (Harper, 1988)
- *The Berenstain Bears and the Missing Dinosaur Bone* by Stan and Jan Berenstain (Random House, 1980)
- *Dinosaurs* by David Lambert (Franklin Watts, 1990)
- *The Dinosaur Who Lived in My Backyard* by B. G. Hennessey (Modern Curriculum, 1990)
- *Danny and the Dinosaur* by Syd Hoff (Harper, 1985)
- *Little Danny Dinosaur* by Janet Craig (Troll, 1988)
- *Dinosaur in Trouble* by Sharon Gordon (Troll, 1980)
- *Dinosaur Alphabet Book* by Patricia Whitehead (Troll, 1985)
- *Story of Dinosaurs* by David Eastman (Troll, 1982)
- *More About Dinosaurs* by David Cutts (Troll, 1982)

Delicious Dinosaur Eggs

Boil extra eggs in a pan of water. Dye the hard-boiled eggs green. Use felt-tipped pens to speckle the eggs. Then place the eggs in a "nest" (a basket filled with real or artificial grass or straw). At snack time, invite children to taste the "dinosaur eggs."

Step out a Stegosaurus

Find out just how long a stegosaurus really was. Place a flag at one end of the playground. Start walking at the flag. Measure, using approximately one small step for every foot. Put a flag at the other end to show the measured length. Then stand back and invite children to look at the flags to see just how long the giant dinosaur was. Repeat for other dinosaurs.

Stegosaurus	20 feet (6 meters)
Apatosaurus	70 feet (21 meters)
Brachiosaurus	90 feet (28 meters)
Triceratops	30 feet (9 meters)
Tyrannosaurus rex	45 feet (14 meters)

Box-o-Saurus

Gather small cardboard boxes, glue, and paper scraps. Have children work in pairs to research, plan, and build a dinosaur model using the boxes. Let them use leftover boxes to make trees and other scenery. You may wish to provide children with paint and brushes to decorate their dinosaurs. Encourage each pair to present its work to the class.

Using the Dinosaur Pattern

- Precut dinosaur patterns from green paper. Have children make dinosaur greeting cards by folding a piece of white paper in half and gluing a dinosaur cutout on the front. Then tell children to write a greeting on the inside of the card and sign it.

- Post pictures of real dinosaurs. On dinosaur cutouts, have children write one or two clues about a specific dinosaur, such as "I have three horns on my head and a bony collar around my neck. Who am I?" Have children trade cutouts. As they read the clues, children should try to guess the name of the dinosaur.

Hot Diggity Dog

Have children pantomime the movement of a puppy as it wags its tail, chews a bone, rolls over, shakes after a bath, digs a hole to bury a bone, or curls up for a nap.

Dog Dishes and Other Wishes

Put pet objects (or pictures of them) in a box: dog collar, bone, brush, ball, leash, water dish, fishnet, fishbowl, birdseed, and a carrot. Have children sort the objects, placing each object that might belong to a dog in one group. Discuss the chosen objects with children and have them tell why it is necessary for a dog owner to have them.

A Dog Named Bingo

Sing "Bingo" with children, inviting them to join in when they can. Sing the song the first time through, spelling the name Bingo. The second time, clap on the letter "B" and sing "I-N-G-O." The third time, clap "B-I" and sing "N-G-O," and so on until all of the letters are clapped rather than sung.

BINGO

There was a farmer had a dog,
And Bingo was his name-o.
B-I-N-G-O, B-I-N-G-O, B-I-N-G-O,
and Bingo was his name-o.

You may wish to sing other familiar songs about dogs. Children will enjoy "How Much Is That Doggie in the Window?," "Oh Where, Oh Where Has My Little Dog Gone?," "Do Your Ears Hang Low?," and "My Dog's Bigger Than Your Dog."

Doggone It!

Recite the following poem with children. Then let them make storyboards to accompany the poem. Write each line of the poem on a separate piece of poster board. Have groups of children illustrate each line. Provide a variety of materials for illustrating: wallpaper, felt, and fabric scraps for the dog; watermelon seeds or birdseed for fleas; and straw, moss, paper, cotton, chalk, paint, and markers for the background and finishing touches.

I'VE GOT A DOG

I've got a dog as thin as a rail
He's got fleas all over his tail;
Every time his tail goes flop,
The fleas on his bottom all hop to his top.

Books to Bark About

Snoopy has long been a favorite with young dog lovers. Ask children to bring in books about this famous dog or about other dogs. To this collection, you may wish to add some of the following titles:

- *Harry the Dirty Dog* by Gene Zion (Harper, 1976)
- *Puppies and Dogs* (Price, Stern, Sloan, 1984)
- *Snoopy's Baseball Game* by Lee Mendelson (Worlds of Wonder, 1986)
- *What a Dog!* by Sharon Gordon (Troll, 1980)
- *You Dirty Dog* by Stephen Caitlin (Troll, 1988)
- *Maxie the Mutt* by Sharon Peters (Troll, 1988)
- *Copycat Dog* by Michael Pellowski (Troll, 1986)

Doggie, Doggie, Where's Your Bone?

Play Doggie, Doggie, Where's Your Bone? Tell children to sit in a circle. Then have one child play the part of the doggie and leave the room. Hide a bone (small wooden block) in a child's hands. Have all children clasp their hands in front of them as though they have the bone. As the doggie returns, have children chant the rhyme:

> Doggie, doggie, where's your bone?
> Somebody took it from your home!
> Doggie, doggie, find your bone.
> Hurry up and bring it home.

The doggie has three guesses to find the bone.

Dandy Dogs

To make a dog, each child will need a paper plate, brown and black construction paper, and two paper brads. Have children cut ears and eyes from the construction paper. Tell them to glue the eyes on the paper-plate head and connect the ears to the head with paper brads. Children can use paper scraps to make additional features or decorations.

Shaggy Dog

Children will enjoy scribbling a shaggy dog, using white chalk on black construction paper. Help them to follow these simple steps:

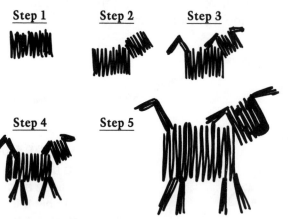

Step 1 **Step 2** **Step 3**

Step 4 **Step 5**

Favorite Dog

Have children take a survey of their friends and relatives to find out the most popular breed of dog. Ask each surveyor to ask as many people as possible to name their favorite dog. Have them record the responses and then share them with the class. Help children graph the responses on a bar graph similar to the one shown.

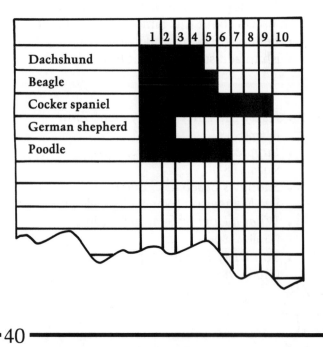

	1	2	3	4	5	6	7	8	9	10
Dachshund										
Beagle										
Cocker spaniel										
German shepherd										
Poodle										

- Make twenty-six dogs. Print one lowercase letter, a–z, on each dog. Then cut twenty-six doghouses from red construction paper. Label the doghouses A–Z. Have children match uppercase and lowercase letters by placing each dog in the correct doghouse.

- Precut five dog patterns. Copy nursery rhymes about dogs on the cutouts and post them in the classroom. Read the rhymes often until children are familiar with the words and rhyming patterns. Include *Hey, Diddle, Diddle* and *Old Mother Hubbard.*

FAIRY TALES

Adopt Some Tales

Provide a rich source of fairy tales, including both individual titles and collections. If possible, display the same fairy tale retold by different authors and illustrated by different artists. Compare the stories and the art. How are they alike? How are they different? You may wish to add the following collections of fairy tales to your personal collection:

- *Treasury of Children's Classics* (Crown, 1987)
- *Tasha Tudor's Book of Fairy Tales* by Tasha Tudor (Putnam, 1988)
- *Little Treasury of Fairy Tales* by Cory Nash (Crown, 1984)
- *Once Upon a Time: A Book of Old-Time Fairy Tales* by Margaret Price (Macmillan, 1986)

Track a Tale

Fairy tales are stories about fairies, dragons, and other make-believe characters. Because they are so much fun, they are told over and over through the years, passing from one generation to the next and from one country to another. As you introduce each new fairy tale, tell children where the tale originated and help them locate the place of origin on a globe.

Tell a Tale

Encourage children to continue the oral tradition by retelling each fairy tale to at least one friend and one family member.

Time for a Tale

After children finish listening to or reading a fairy tale, have them create a sandwich board to advertise it. At the end of the unit, have children wear the sandwich boards as they parade through the halls.

Red Hen Helps Herself

Read or retell *The Little Red Hen*, an English fairy tale. Discuss how Red Hen felt when no one would help her. Let children share how they feel when they have an idea for a game or an activity but can't get anyone to help them.

Puppet Pals for Red Hen

Cut the fingers off an old glove. Have children use marking pens, felt scraps, sequins, and pom-poms to make a "handful" of puppets. Tell children to make puppets for Red Hen, a chick, a duck, a cat, and a dog and use them for retelling *The Little Red Hen*.

Red Hen Needs Help

Help children write help wanted advertisements to put in the newspaper. Post the finished ads in the room.

> **WANTED:** Baker
> **TO DO:** Bake homemade bread
> **APPLY IN PERSON TO THE LITTLE RED HEN**

The Three Billy Goats Gruff

Read or retell the Norwegian fairy tale *The Three Billy Goats Gruff*. Have children work together to write a letter from the troll to the goats, in which they explain why the troll does not want the goats trip-trapping on his bridge.

Goat Thumbprints

Have children use an inkpad to make fingerprints and then draw a goat face on each print to represent each of the goats in *The Three Billy Goats Gruff*.

Goat Masks

Cut goat faces from tagboard. Cut large openings for the eyes. Attach ribbon or string to the sides so the masks can be tied around children's heads. Let children paint the masks. Then use them for acting out the story.

The Gingerbread Man

Read or retell different versions of *The Gingerbread Man*, an American fairy tale. Then let children make gingerbread men cookies. Help them roll prepared dough onto wax paper and cut the dough into the shape of a gingerbread man and bake. Have children decorate the cookies with raisins, currants, cinnamon candies, and icing.

Gingerbread Man Movie

Help children plan and present a play based on *The Gingerbread Man*. Assign parts for each character. Use a paper bag to make a costume for the Gingerbread Man. Use clothes brought from home as costumes for other characters. Have children plan and rehearse their lines and movements. Then, as children present the play, videotape it for their viewing later.

Gingerbread Match

Cut twelve gingerbread men from tagboard. Decorate pairs of the cutouts exactly the same. Mix the cutouts and let children match the identical pairs.

The Three Bears

Read or retell the English fairy tale *The Three Bears*. Then have the class write an invitation from Mama Bear to Goldilocks, inviting her to have porridge with her family.

Bears' Big Production

Help children plan and present a puppet show for *The Three Bears*. Make the three bears from paper bags. Make Goldilocks from a wooden spoon and yarn. Let the puppeteers practice their parts before presenting the show to the class.

Jeers and Cheers for Goldilocks

Have children create cue cards to go along with the puppet show. Cards should get the audience involved in the puppet show by making suggestions for various sound effects. Here are some examples:

| creeeak | slurrrp | bang! |
| GRRR | snore | clap |

- Distribute cutout patterns of each character. Tell children to write the name of the character at the top of the cutout. Then have them write words that tell something about the character.

- Precut eight to ten of each character pattern. Have children select a cutout and on it write a letter to that character.

- Provide cutout patterns of each character. Have children write events from each story that are obviously real and ones that are obviously make-believe.

- Provide cutout patterns of each character. Tell children to write on the cutouts two or three sentences telling what they thought of each story. Post the "reviews" on the class bulletin board for all to share.

FAMILIES

Family Play

Make a house using a large box or a sheet over a card table. Provide both adult and child-sized clothes for a dress-up play. Provide vehicles (tricycles, wagons, toy cars) for traveling to work or for shopping. Encourage dramatic play.

Family Fun

Invite parents and grandparents to visit the classroom. Encourage them to bring pictures of themselves as children and to be prepared to share some of their own childhood experiences. Let visitors pose with their children for a family portrait. Display the photographs on the classroom bulletin board.

Family Trees

Make a family forest. Cover a wall with butcher paper. Cut out a paper tree trunk for each child. Glue the trunks on the butcher paper. Invite children to cut out a leaf for each member of their family, including grandparents. Draw or paste a photograph of each family member on individual leaves and then glue them to the tree.

Family Postcards

Cut rectangles from tagboard. On one side of the postcard, have children draw a picture that shows an activity they enjoy with their families. On the back, have them write or dictate a message or greeting to their families. If possible, address and mail the postcards.

The Families on the Bus

Sing "The Wheels on the Bus" with children. Make up additional verses that include each member of the family.

THE WHEELS ON THE BUS

The wheels on the bus go round and round,
Round and round, round and round.
The wheels on the bus go round and round,
All through the town.

2. The babies on the bus go waa, waa, waa

3. The daddies on the bus go shhh, shhh, shhh

Family of Ducks

Read *Make Way for Ducklings* by Robert McCloskey. Invite volunteers to take the parts of Mr. and Mrs. Mallard. As you reread the story, have volunteers pantomime the actions and reactions of the parents.

Reading Is Family Fun

Invite children to bring their make-believe families (stuffed bears, toy rabbits, dolls) to the reading area in the classroom. Let them get their "families" settled before beginning to read. Be sure to include a variety of books about families and family life.

- *Are You My Mother?* by P.D. Eastman (Random House, 1986)
- *The Perfect Family* by Nancy Carlson (Carolrhoda Books, 1985)
- *Nobody Asked Me If I Wanted a Baby Sister* by Martha Alexander (Dial, 1971)
- *Ask Mr. Bear* by Marjorie Flack (Macmillan, 1986)
- *Mama, Daddy, Baby and Me* by Lisa Gewing (Spirit, 1989)
- *Grandpa and Bo* by Kevin Henkes (Greenwillow, 1986)

Mother, May I?

Demonstrate "baby steps" and "giant steps." Then play Mother, May I? Choose one child to be Mother. Other children line up thirty feet in front of Mother. The object of the game is to reach Mother first.

Mother tells one of the children how many and what kind of steps to take. The child must ask, "Mother, may I?" and wait for a "yes" answer before he or she moves. If the child forgets, he or she must go back to the starting line. Even if the question is asked, Mother may say "no."

Parents and People

Sing or read the words to "Parents Are People" by Carol Hall from *Free to Be . . . You and Me* by Marlo Thomas. List the jobs mothers have. Brainstorm other jobs that mothers can have and add them to the list. Repeat for the jobs fathers can have. Invite volunteers to illustrate each job on the list.

Using the Family Patterns

- Staple five people-shaped pages together to make a book. Let children make a family album.

- Distribute cutouts. Help children to make puppets by decorating cutouts and by gluing on craft sticks. Use the puppets for acting out favorite poems and nursery rhymes about families.

- Give children cutouts to correspond to the members of their families. On each cutout have them write all the words they can think of to describe that family member.

- Invite children to use the cutouts to tell a story of their own about a family.

49

FISH
And Other Sea Creatures

Fishing for a Good Book?
Begin a discussion about fish by sharing Helen Palmer's book *A Fish Out of Water*. After reading the book, talk about things a fish needs to stay alive and what may happen if a pet fish gets too much of a good thing.

You may wish to add these titles to your sea of books.

- *Blue Sea* by Robert Kalan (Greenwillow, 1979)
- *A Fish Out of Water* by Helen Palmer (Random House, 1961)
- *Fish Is Fish* by Leo Lionni (Pantheon, 1970)
- *Louis the Fish* by Arthur Yorinks (Farrar, Straus and Giroux, 1980)
- *Swimmy* by Leo Lionni (Pantheon, 1973)
- *What Is a Fish?* by David Eastman (Troll, 1982)

Favorite Fish
Let children mold, bend, pinch, and roll clay to make replicas of their favorite fish. Display the models on an "ocean" of light blue cloth.

Crab Walk
Have children sit with their feet flat on the floor. Have them lean back on their hands. Then have them move forward, backward, or sideways, keeping their backs as straight and level as possible.

Shark Shapes

Help children to bend pipe cleaners to make the outline of a shark. Then have them line one side of the pipe cleaner with glue and put the shark on a sheet of tissue paper. When dry, tell them to trim away the tissue from the outside edge of the shark and use tissue scraps to add eyes or other details. Hang the sharks on a window or from the ceiling so that light can pass through them.

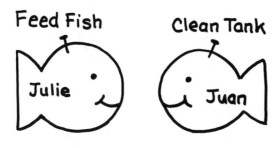

Fish as Pets

You will need:
    tank
    1/2 gallon (2 liters) of rainwater for
        every fish
    water plants (eelgrass or duckweed
        is best)
    gravel or sand
    a few snails
    store-bought fish food

Cover the bottom of the tank with gravel. Place a few plants in the gravel. Fill the tank with rainwater and then add a few snails (to keep the tank clean) and fresh-water fish like guppies and goldfish.

Check with a pet store owner to see how much food the fish need. Have children take turns feeding the fish and cleaning the tank.

Fish Pictionary

Provide a piece of white paper for each child. Brainstorm names of fish found in either fresh water or salt water. Let each child draw and label one of the fish on the paper. Put the pictures in alphabetical order. Have volunteers make a cover for the *Fish Pictionary.* To finish the book, staple together the cover and the pages.

Fish Rhymes

Help children memorize the following rhyme.

FISH ALIVE

1, 2, 3, 4, 5,
I caught a fish alive.
6, 7, 8, 9, 10,
I let him go again.
Why did I let him go?
Because he bit my finger so!

Make a list of words that rhyme with *five, ten,* and *go.* Use the words to create other fish rhymes using "Fish Alive" as a pattern. Make sure that lines 1 and 2, lines 3 and 4, and lines 5 and 6 rhyme.

FISH ALIVE

1, 2, 3, 4, 5,

_____

6, 7, 8, 9, 10,

_____

Why did I let him go?

_____

Fabulous Fish

Children will need two paper plates each. Help them cut one plate into four equal sections. Use two pieces for fins and two for the tail.

Funny, Funny Fish

Invite children to write riddles about sea animals. Have them use at least two facts in each riddle. For example:

It has eight legs.
It can change colors from white to
  yellow to red to brown.
It can walk and swim.
What is it?   *(octopus)*

I have 5 legs and a shell. What am I? (starfish)

Sea Collage

Have children cut pictures of sea creatures from old magazines. Cover a bulletin board with the pictures to make a sea collage. Have children compare sizes, shapes, and colors of sea creatures displayed. Talk about some of their unusual features, such as claws, shells, horns, tentacles, wings, and teeth.

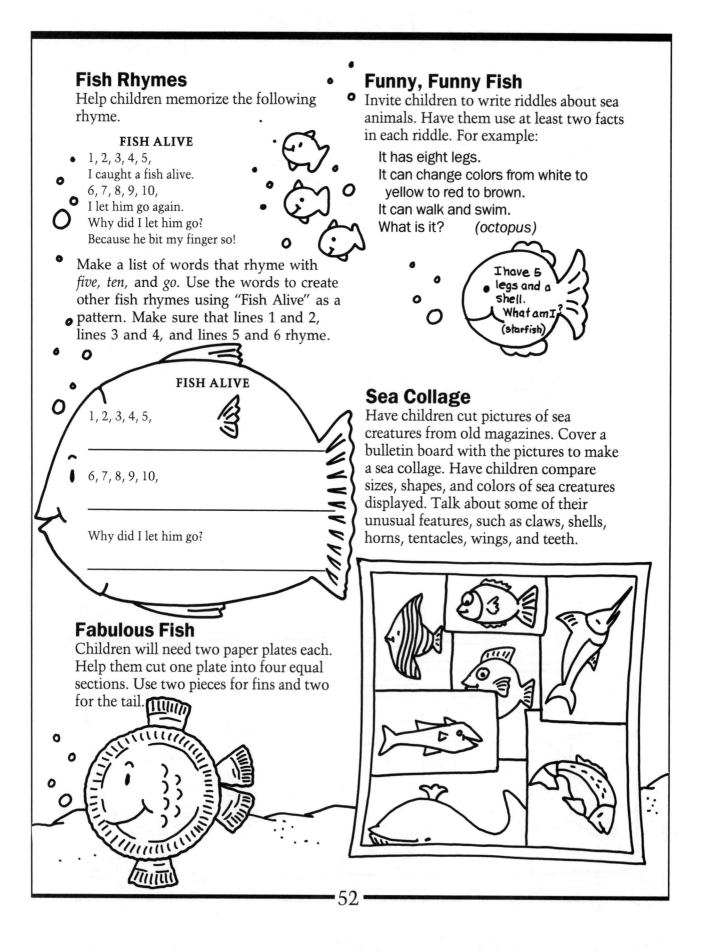

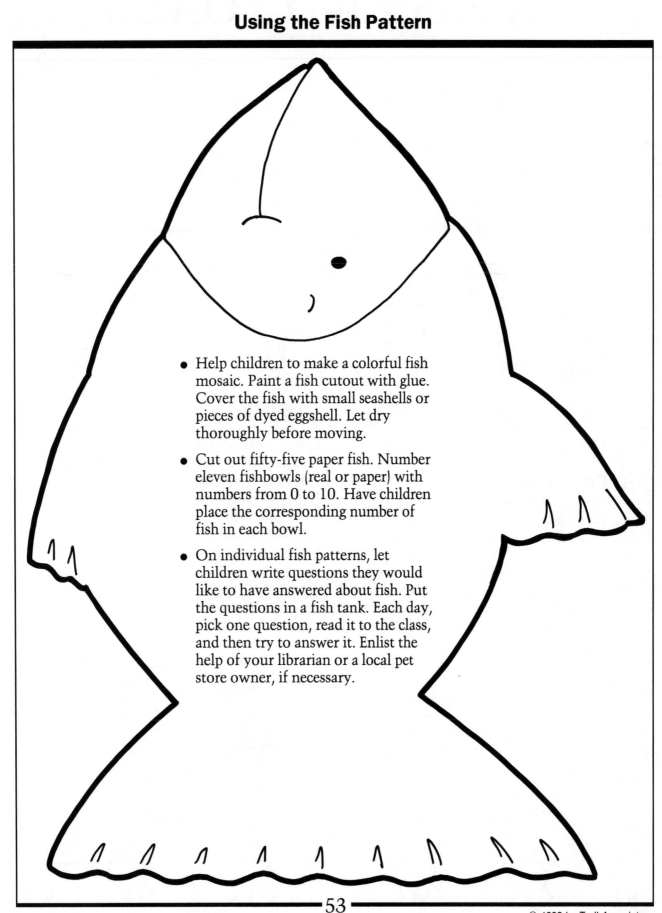

- Help children to make a colorful fish mosaic. Paint a fish cutout with glue. Cover the fish with small seashells or pieces of dyed eggshell. Let dry thoroughly before moving.

- Cut out fifty-five paper fish. Number eleven fishbowls (real or paper) with numbers from 0 to 10. Have children place the corresponding number of fish in each bowl.

- On individual fish patterns, let children write questions they would like to have answered about fish. Put the questions in a fish tank. Each day, pick one question, read it to the class, and then try to answer it. Enlist the help of your librarian or a local pet store owner, if necessary.

FROGS AND TOADS

There's a Frog on a Log

Sing this add-on song about a frog in the sea.

There's a Hole in the Middle of the Sea

There's a hole in the middle of the sea,
There's a hole in the middle of the sea,
There'a a hole, there's a hole,
There's a hole in the middle of the sea.

(2) There's a log in the hole in the middle of the sea
(3) There's a bump on the log in the hole in the middle of the sea
(4) There's a frog on the bump . . .
(5) There's a fly on the frog . . .
(6) There's a wing on the fly . . .
(7) There's a flea on the wing . . .

Sing other familiar songs about frogs, such as "A Frog Went A-Courtin'" and Kermit the Frog's "It's Not Easy Bein' Green."

Frog in Your Throat

Help children to make frog puppets. Have them paint one side of a paper plate red and the other side green. When dry, tell them to fold the plate in half with the red part inside. Next have them cut out paper eyes and legs and glue them on the plate. Let children entertain the class by having their frog puppets sing their favorite songs.

Leapfrog

Play leapfrog with children. Have them crouch, one behind the other, with the heads tucked inward toward their bodies. Have the "frog" at the back of the line leap over each of the other "frogs" until he or she reaches the front of the line. Repeat, until all children have had an opportunity to play.

As a variation, divide the class into two teams and play leapfrog as a relay race.

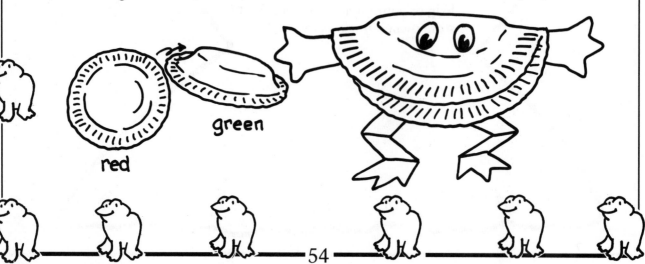

red

green

Frog Jump

Have children squat, with their hands on the floor in front of them. When you say, "Jump, frogs, jump!" have children jump forward like frogs, landing on their hands and feet at the same time.

Frog Paperweight

Have children paint stones green. Tell them to use markers to add details to the frog paperweights. If they wish, children may glue the frogs on lily pads made from green paper.

Frog Friends

Let children use a small net to gather some tadpoles. Put them in a gallon (5- liter) jar of pond water and display them in the Science Center. Observe the tadpoles daily. Encourage children to keep journals, drawing pictures and writing descriptions of the changes that occur. (Be sure to add a green, leafy vegetable or two as food for the growing tadpoles. Have children return them to the pond when they've finished their observations.)

Tell a Tale of Tadpoles

Have four volunteers paint cards to show the life cycle of a frog: egg, tadpole without legs, tadpole with legs, frog. Help children arrange the cards to show the correct sequence.

Day 1
I see 3 tadpoles without legs.

Day 7
1 tadpole has legs now.

Day 9
2 tadpoles have legs now.

Follow the Frog

Play in the same manner as follow the leader. Choose one child to be the leader, who will then suggest a direction such as "Hop on one foot," "Hop to the right," or "Hop around your desk." All the other "frogs" must follow the leader's directions.

Frogs and Toads

Have children compare real frogs and toads. Explain that although most people have a hard time telling them apart, there are differences. Frogs are smooth and moist; toads are dry and bumpy. Can children find other differences? Write children's observations on a comparison chart like the one shown below.

FROGS	TOADS
Smooth and moist	Dry and bumpy
Long legs	Shorter legs
Have some teeth	No teeth
Medium weight	Fatter than frogs
Take long jumps	Take shorter jumps

Finding out About Frogs

Cut out paper lily pads. Place them on the floor, leading to a shelf or table where books about frogs and toads are displayed. Let children follow the lily pads to the books during independent reading time. You might also wish to write the book titles on the lily pads. After reading the books, children can tell about their favorite part of the book. Write their responses on the corresponding lily pad.

Here are some hopping good books about frogs and toads:

- *Frog and Toad Are Friends* by Arnold Lobel (Harper, 1970)
- *Discovering Frogs* by Douglas Florian (Macmillan, 1986)
- *Can You Jump Like a Frog?* by Marc Brown (Dutton, 1989)
- *Freddie the Frog* by Rose Greydanus (Troll, 1980)
- *Frog on His Own* by Mercer Mayer (Dial, 1973)

Using the Frog Pattern

- Some frogs can jump up to twenty times their own length. Measure how far each child can jump and record the length on a frog pattern.

- Write each child's name on a separate frog pattern. Place the names, as appropriate, on a bulletin board entitled "Something to Hop About," which features good work or good citizenship.

- Precut twelve to fifteen patterns from green paper. Have children draw or cut and paste pictures of objects whose names begin with the consonant cluster *fr* as in *frog*.

- On frog-shaped paper, have children write stories about one day in the life of a frog. If they wish, they can illustrate their stories.

FUNNY CHARACTERS

Amelia Bedelia

Invite children to join you on the reading rug or at another comfortable place in the room to read *Amelia Bedelia* by Peggy Parish. Show them a picture of Amelia Bedelia. Explain that Amelia Bedelia has been left alone on her first day of work to tidy up Mrs. Rogers's house. Then share the hilarious things that happen as Amelia Bedelia sets about her duties.

Side-Splitting Amelia

Have children draw a picture of Amelia Bedelia and something she did that strikes them as funny. Let each child share his or her work with the class.

Literal-Minded Amelia

Have children explain what "drawing the drapes" means. Then have them tell what Amelia Bedelia thought the directions meant and why her actions were funny.

Help children understand the humor in other actions taken by Amelia Bedelia by having them explain both the intended meaning and the literal meaning of each of the following directions:

- change the towels
- put the lights out
- dress the chicken
- dust the furniture
- measure the rice
- trim the fat

Amelia Bedelia Thinking

Let children work with partners to think of other directions that would be funny if taken literally. Have them write the directions on paper and illustrate them.

Amelia Bedelia Books

If children enjoyed *Amelia Bedelia*, encourage them to read other books about the character.

- *Thank You, Amelia Bedelia* by Peggy Parish (Harper, 1964)
- *Amelia Bedelia and the Surprise Shower* by Peggy Parish (Harper, 1979)
- *Come Back, Amelia Bedelia* by Peggy Parish (Harper, 1970)

Curious George

Read H. A. Rey's *Curious George Rides a Bike* to the children. Have children tell about things the author wrote that made them laugh. Ask them to point out specific things in the illustrations that were funny.

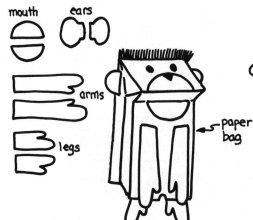

Curious George Investigates

Have a volunteer retell the part of the story where Curious George makes a fleet of boats. Ask why this was funny and what Curious George wanted to find out.

Help children fold newspapers to make boats just like Curious George's. Have them experiment with a tub of water to see if the paper boats float.

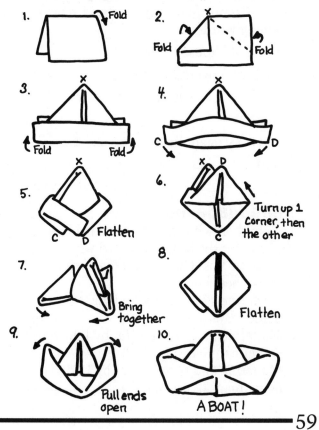

1. Fold
2. Fold   Fold   Fold
3. Fold   Fold
4. C   D
5. Flatten   C   D
6. Turn up 1 corner, then the other
7. Bring together
8. Flatten
9. Pull ends open
10. A BOAT!

Curious George Puppets

Have children make paper-bag puppets of Curious George. Use the puppets to act out the story. You may wish to create a stage by hanging a sheet across a door or draping a sheet over a chair. To make the puppet, follow these steps:

1. Cut parts from construction paper.
2. Glue the mouth parts on the bag as shown.
3. Draw eyes and a nose on the flap.
4. Glue on ears, feet and arms.
5. Cut and glue fringe for the monkey's hair.

mouth   ears   arms   legs   paper bag

Curious About Curious George

If children are curious about what other mischief Curious George gets into, have them check out and read the following books about the character:

- *Curious George* by H. A. Rey (Houghton Mifflin, 1973)
- *Curious George Gets a Medal* by H. A. Rey (Houghton Mifflin, 1957)
- *Curious George Flies a Kite* by H. A. Rey and Margaret Rey (Houghton Mifflin, 1977)
- *Curious George Goes to the Hospital* by H. A. Rey and Margaret Rey (Houghton Mifflin, 1973)

Madeline

To set the stage for reading *Madeline* by Ludwig Bemelmans, have children sit in two straight lines. Wrap a dark sheet or cape around yourself and cover your head with a dark cloth. Introduce yourself as Miss Clavel. Then read the book to children.

Let children share the things that Madeline did that they thought were funny. Show the picture in the book that accompanies each event.

Make Me Madeline

Children will enjoy acting out the story. Have a volunteer play the part of Madeline. Have eleven other children play the girls in the story. Have one child take the part of Miss Clavel and one take the part of the doctor.

Provide a box of dress-up clothes, including a variety of hats and dresses. Help each actor find an appropriate costume. Help children to find or improvise props necessary for their parts. Set the stage for actors by suggesting sections of the classroom to be the bedroom, town square, and hospital.

Then reread the story, having the actors pantomime their roles. Choose other children to play each role and repeat until everyone has played a role.

Make Madeline

Demonstrate and then have children arrange and glue paper circles, rectangles, and triangles to make Madeline.

Encourage children to write or dictate a new adventure for Madeline. Have them refer to the picture of Madeline to illustrate the story.

Rhyme for Madeline

Copy these words from the story on the board. Complete the sentences with new rhyming words.

In an old house in Paris

that was covered with vines

lived twelve little girls in two straight lines.

In two straight lines they _____

and _____ and _____.

More Madeline

For children who would like to read more about the funny little girl who lived with Miss Clavel, you may wish to suggest these books:

- *Madeline's Rescue* by Ludwig Bemelmans (Penguin, 1977)
- *Madeline and the Bad Hat* by Ludwig Bemelmans (Penguin, 1977)
- *Madeline and the Gypsies* by Ludwig Bemelmans (Penguin, 1977)

60

Using the Character Patterns

- Use the cutouts as postcards on which children can write notes to the school librarian to find out the titles of other books about the funny characters.

- Precut a Curious George pattern for each child. On the pattern have children write about a time they were curious about something. Be sure to have them tell what happened.

- Copy the patterns onto paper and cut them out. Use the characters as a border around a bulletin board in the reading center or library.

MONKEYS

Monkey See, Monkey Do

Play "Monkey See, Monkey Do" in the same way you would play Follow the Leader, having the class copy the actions or funny antics of a child chosen to be the leader.

Monkey Matters

Display pictures of real monkeys. Name each monkey shown and talk about its physical characteristics, habitat, and diet. Invite children to share what they know about monkeys or adventures they experienced while visiting monkeys at the zoo.

Monkey Walk

Explain that monkeys use both their arms and their legs to walk or run. If possible, observe a real monkey as it walks or demonstrate the monkey walk for the class. Then ask children to walk like monkeys. Play music from Disney's *Jungle Book* record or other lively, junglelike music while children practice the monkey walk.

Monkey with a Good Book

Swing into the mood with these wonderful books about monkeys:
- *Caps for Sale* by Esphyr Slobodkina (Harper, 1947)
- *Trouble Is His Name* by Elizabeth Montgomery (Garrard, 1976)
- *Monkeys* by Patricia Whitehead (Troll, 1982)
- *The Monkey and the Crocodile* by Paul Galdone (Houghton Mifflin, 1979)
- *Curious George* by H.A. Rey (Houghton Mifflin, 1973)

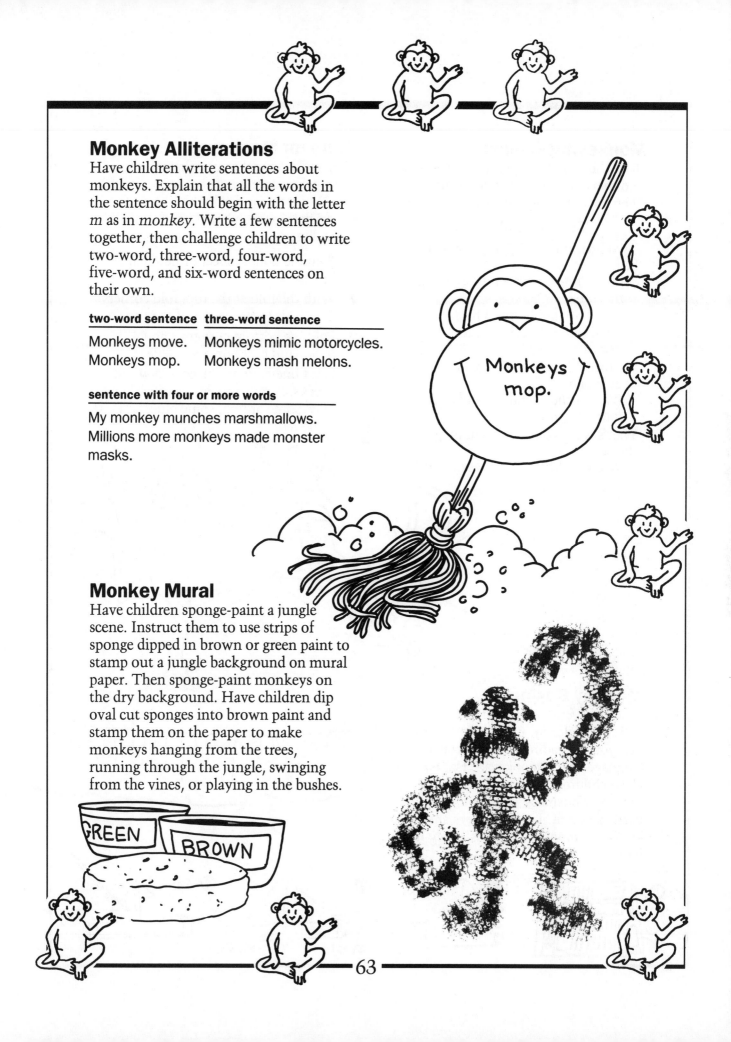

Monkey Alliterations

Have children write sentences about monkeys. Explain that all the words in the sentence should begin with the letter *m* as in *monkey.* Write a few sentences together, then challenge children to write two-word, three-word, four-word, five-word, and six-word sentences on their own.

two-word sentence	three-word sentence
Monkeys move.	Monkeys mimic motorcycles.
Monkeys mop.	Monkeys mash melons.

sentence with four or more words

My monkey munches marshmallows.
Millions more monkeys made monster masks.

Monkeys mop.

Monkey Mural

Have children sponge-paint a jungle scene. Instruct them to use strips of sponge dipped in brown or green paint to stamp out a jungle background on mural paper. Then sponge-paint monkeys on the dry background. Have children dip oval cut sponges into brown paint and stamp them on the paper to make monkeys hanging from the trees, running through the jungle, swinging from the vines, or playing in the bushes.

GREEN

BROWN

Monkeying Around

Share the finger play with children. Read it to them and demonstrate the motions. Then have them join in as you repeat it.

Two Little Monkeys

Two little monkeys, jumping on the bed,
(Two index fingers doing jumping motion.)
One fell off and bumped his head.
(One index finger falls, then taps head.)
We took him to the doctor and the doctor said:
(Wrap other hand around hurt index finger.)
That's what you get for jumping on the bed!
(Shake other index finger.)

Monkey Business

Read *Caps for Sale* by Esphyr Slobodkina with the children. Encourage them to join you in reading the predictable language of the monkeys: "tsz, tsz, tsz!" Have children explain what kind of "monkey business" the monkeys participated in. Let volunteers share kinds of "monkey business" they have participated in.

Caps for Monkeys

Help children make paper hats to use as props when acting out the story *Caps for Sale.* You will need a double sheet of newspaper for each hat. Then follow these directions:

1. Fold the double sheet of newspaper in half.
2. With the fold at the top, fold corners 1 and 2 into the center of the paper.
3. Fold the bottom corners 3 and 4 (front and back) up and staple.
4. Paint one hat with black and white checks. Paint some of the other hats gray, some brown, some blue, and some red.

① ② Fold Fold 2 3 4 ③ staple staple ④ Paint

Using the Monkey Pattern

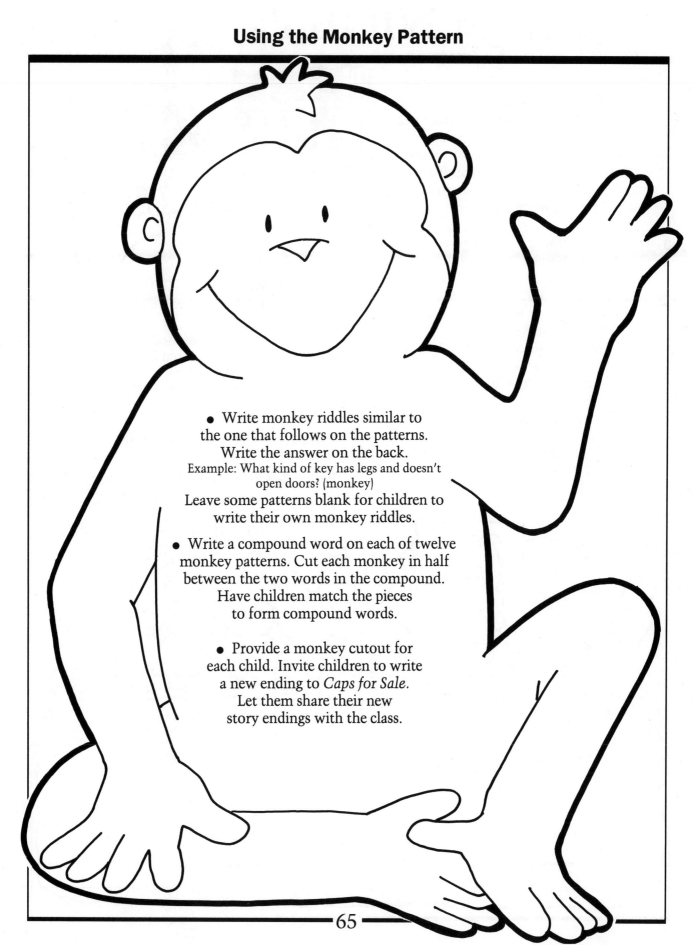

- Write monkey riddles similar to the one that follows on the patterns. Write the answer on the back.

  Example: What kind of key has legs and doesn't open doors? (monkey)

  Leave some patterns blank for children to write their own monkey riddles.

- Write a compound word on each of twelve monkey patterns. Cut each monkey in half between the two words in the compound. Have children match the pieces to form compound words.

- Provide a monkey cutout for each child. Invite children to write a new ending to *Caps for Sale*. Let them share their new story endings with the class.

Nighttime Books

Invite children to sit on the floor near you. Darken the room to resemble nighttime. Read classic books about people and animals at night. Include as many of the following titles in your reading as possible.

- *Goodnight Moon* by Margaret W. Brown (Harper, 1947)
- *Good-Night, Owl!* by Pat Hutchins (Macmillan, 1972)
- *Ira Sleeps Over* by Bernard Waber (Houghton Mifflin, 1975)
- *There's a Nightmare in My Closet* by Mercer Mayer (Dial, 1968)
- *Bedtime for Frances* by Russell Hoban (Harper, 1960)
- *The Nighttime Book* by Mauri Kunnas (Crown, 1985)
- *Bedtime Story* by Rose Greydanus (Troll, 1988)

Nighttime Play

Sing the song "Ten in the Bed" with children.

Ten in the Bed

Verse 1.   There were ten in the bed and the little one said, "Roll over, roll over!" So they all rolled over and one fell out.

Verse 2.   There were nine in the bed . . .

Verses 3–9. (Count one less each verse.)

Verse 10.   There was one on the bed and the little one said, "Good night."

Night Is a Nice Time

Encourage children to talk about their own nighttime experiences. Emphasize the pleasant aspects of nighttime, such as taking a bubble bath, counting the stars, watching the moon come out, snuggling with a parent and being read to, and getting rest. Let children draw pictures to illustrate something they enjoy about nighttime. Post the pictures on a bulletin board covered with black paper.

Night Workers

Explain to children that although most people are awake during the day and sleep at night, some people work at night to keep other people safe and healthy or to provide a service that is better done at that time. Brainstorm jobs that people do at night. List the people and their jobs on a chart.

Nighttime Noises

Have children close their eyes and recall noises they have heard at night. Ask them to talk about who or what made each noise.

Night Workers

Person	Job
doctor/nurse	helps people who are sick
grocery worker	puts food on the shelves
police officer	protects us while we sleep
fire fighter	watches over our homes
driver/pilot	makes deliveries/flights
baker	bakes bread
sanitation worker	cleans streets

Good Night!

Tell about a time when you were little and weren't sure if you wanted to spend the night away from home. Invite children to share similar experiences. Then read *Ira Sleeps Over* by Bernard Waber. Have children talk about how Ira solved the sleepover problem.

Nighttime Rituals

Talk about things children do to get ready for bed. Then sing "This Is the Way We Go to Bed" to the tune of "Mulberry Bush." Have children pantomime each action as you sing. Invite children to add more verses to the song.

THIS IS THE WAY WE GO TO BED

This is the way we go to bed,
Go to bed, go to bed,
This is the way we go to bed
At bedtime in the evening.
2. This is the way we take a bath . . .
3. This is the way we brush our teeth . . .
4. This is the way Dad reads to us . . .
5. This is the way we say "Good night" . . .

What Causes Nighttime?

Use a globe and a flashlight ("sun") to demonstrate what causes darkness at nighttime. Point out the place where you live on the globe. Turn the globe so that the flashlight shines on the place you live. Point out how the sun makes light. Leave the sun in a fixed position, shining down on the earth. Have a child slowly turn the earth on its axis, making the place where you live turn away from the sun. Invite children to explain what happens. Then have them watch to see what happens as the earth continues to turn, moving the place where you live back toward the sun.

● Provide each child with a piece of paper shaped like a crescent moon. Ask them to think about dreams they have had and to draw a picture of their favorite dream.

● Write the words to the following nursery rhymes on individual moon patterns. Recite the rhymes with children at appropriate times during the day.
"Wee Willie Winkie"
"Wynken, Blynken, and Nod"
"Star Light, Star Bright"
"The Man in the Moon"
"The Old Woman Tossed up in a
    Basket"

● Precut moon patterns. On each cutout, have children write compound words that relate to night, such as *bedtime, sunset, nighttime, nightgown, and midnight.*

Humpty Dumpty Darlings

Recite "Humpty Dumpty" with children. Then ask them to decorate hard-boiled eggs to represent Humpty Dumpty. Provide marking pens, yarn, glue, fabric scraps, and ribbon.

Horns for Little Boy Blue

Say the rhyme "Little Boy Blue." Invite children to join in. Then help children to make horns for Little Boy Blue to use to call the sheep and the cow. Paint a cardboard tube. Fasten a piece of waxed paper to one end of the tube with a rubber band. Punch holes in the tube with a pencil. To play the horn, hum into the open end while covering different holes.

Humpty Dumpty Dozen

Have children put eggs into an egg carton. Tell them to count the eggs in the full carton to discover how many eggs are in a dozen.

WAXED PAPER

Jack and Jill Opposites

Chant the words to "Jack and Jill" to the children. Have them repeat the words after you. Write the words *up* and *down* on the board. Have children suggest and pantomime other pairs of opposites.

Little Miss Muffet

Recite the words to "Little Miss Muffet" with the children. Then sing the words to the tune of "Nobody Likes Me."

Help for Miss Muffet

Have children think of something that might have made Little Miss Muffet's situation less frightening. (Sample answers: she could have gotten rid of the spider by spraying it with bug spray or by capturing it in a box.)

Nursery Rhyme Day

Plan a day to celebrate nursery rhymes and nursery rhyme characters.

- Decorate the entrance to your classroom with full-sized nursery rhyme characters drawn or painted by the children.

- Invite children to dress up as their favorite nursery rhyme character. Provide a box of props and costume bits for children to use. Include a variety of hats, old dresses and pants, aprons, musical instruments, stuffed animals, and the like.

- Have a nursery rhyme parade. Children can march from room to room wearing their costumes, holding posters on which they have written and illustrated their favorite nursery rhymes, or chanting favorite rhymes.

- Invite a storyteller to come and share his or her favorite nursery rhymes.

- Duplicate the words to the children's favorite rhymes. Let children staple the pages together and make a cover for the booklet.

- Invite volunteers to act out their favorite rhyme and have the others guess the rhyme.

- Put on a radio show. Provide a lectern (box or table) and a microphone. Have a moderator introduce each group of children. Then have the children take parts and present their favorite nursery rhyme "on the air."

Using the Character Patterns

- Punch two finger-sized holes in the bottom of each pattern. Have children place their pointer and index fingers through the holes to resemble the character's legs. Children may use the patterns as puppets for acting out the rhymes.

- On precut patterns of each character, have children write questions they would like to ask the character.

- Cover several Humpty Dumpty cutouts with glue. Place pieces of dyed eggshell over the glue to make the character's face and clothes. Decorate the classroom with the cutouts.

- Precut one pattern for each character. Write a rhyming pair of words from the rhyme on the pattern. Have children think of other rhyming words. Write them on the pattern.

73

PEOPLE IN OUR NEIGHBORHOOD

My Neighborhood

Help children make a model neighborhood out of boxes, using large boxes for houses, schools, stores, fire stations, and the like. Tell children to stack boxes to make tall buildings. Then have them add details with paint, crayons, and construction paper.

Getting Around the Neighborhood

Provide toy cars, toy trucks, and tricycles to encourage dramatic play in the model neighborhood. Have volunteers make stop signs and traffic lights out of poster board and add them to the play area.

A Song About Your Neighborhood

Have children sing the Sesame Street song "People in Your Neighborhood." Tell them to hold up a picture of each worker as he or she is mentioned in the song.

People Posters

Have children brainstorm a list of people who work in their neighborhood. Then trace the outline of each child on mural paper. Have children use the outlines to draw and cut out life-size pictures of the workers. Encourage them to draw the appropriate clothing and some tools necessary for their worker. Post the pictures in the hallway outside your classroom.

Busy People

Read books about people in your neighborhood and the jobs they do.

- *Richard Scarry's Busiest People Ever* by Richard Scarry (Random House, 1976)
- *What's It Like to Be a Doctor* by Judith Bauer (Troll, 1990)
- *What's It Like to Be a Nurse* by Judith Bauer (Troll, 1990)
- *What's It Like to Be a Teacher* by Kira Daniel (Troll, 1989)
- *What's It Like to Be a Veterinarian* by Judith Stamper (Troll, 1990)
- *When We Grow Up* by Anne Rockwell (Dutton, 1981)
- *Who Does What?* by Eric Hill (Price, Stern, Sloan, 1982)

Fire Fighter Finger Puppets

Help children to make a fire fighter
finger puppet. Have them cut one 1 1/2
inch × 2 1/2 inch (3 3/4 cm x 6 1/4 cm) oval and
one 3 inch × 1 inch (7 1/2 cm x 2 1/2 cm)
rectangle from red felt. Then tell them to
roll and glue the short ends of the
rectangle around their pointer finger to
make a coat. Have children fold the oval
in half, cut a semicircle on the fold, and
put the oval hat on top of the fire
fighter's head. Use a black pen to draw a
face on the child's finger. Have children
use the finger puppets to act out a finger
play.

Hats for Fire Fighters

Help children make fire fighters' hats.
Let them use the hats for dramatic play.

22"
(56 cm)

CUT

FOLD

17" (43 cm)

Doctors and Nurses

Discuss with children how some workers
in the neighborhood keep people healthy.
Children might enjoy reading about
some of these workers in *Curious George
Goes to the Hospital* by H. A. Rey.
Point out the "tools" used by the doctors
and nurses in the book. Then let children
take turns playing "doctor" and "nurse."
Suggest that their patients be stuffed
animals or other favorite toys.

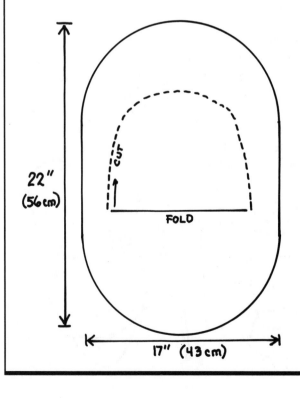

Doctor's Office

Have one or two adult volunteers help you set up a mock doctor's office in your room. Borrow a scale for weighing the children, a tape measure for measuring their height, an eye chart for checking their vision. Invite children to come for a "checkup." Record the findings.

Police Officers on Duty

Play a version of Red Light, Green Light. Have one child play the role of a police officer directing traffic. The child will need a police hat, a whistle, and a sign. One side of the sign should be red with STOP written on it. The other side of the sign should be green with GO. Have the other children walk when the officer directs them with the green sign; have them stop when the officer displays the red sign. Tell the officer that he or she may blow the whistle at offenders. Children will enjoy issuing traffic tickets to repeat offenders.

Police Officer Mobile

Help children to make a mobile. Use tagboard to draw and cut out a police officer. Hang from the officer pictures of tools, equipment, and special clothing needed for the job.

Carpenter

Provide wood, nails, hammers, screws, and screwdrivers. Under your close supervision, have children plan and build simple objects such as stools, birdhouses, or boxes.

Baker

Have children play the role of a baker. Help them to dip refrigerator biscuits in melted butter and then roll them in cinnamon and sugar. Children will enjoy baking and eating the treats they have made. Provide help with the baking and cooling of the biscuits.

Using the
Police Officer Pattern

- Tell children to collect newspaper articles about police officers performing their duties. Collect the articles and glue each one on a separate pattern. Read the articles to the class and discuss with them the variety of duties police officers perform. You may wish to create a bulletin board around this theme.

- Precut six patterns. Have children help you print class rules on the cutouts. Post the rules in the classroom.

- Trace and cut out one police officer and post it on the bulletin board. Encourage children to write tickets for silly violations and then post the tickets around the police officer. One example of a violation might be, "You ate too much spaghetti today. Your fine is 1¢ for every noodle over twenty that you ate."

SEASONS

Seasonal Changes

Tell children that they are going to adopt a tree. Explain that they are going to observe the tree once a week, watching for seasonal changes in the leaves and the bark of the tree. (Seasonal changes will depend on where you live.) Help children to make diaries in which to record their observations. Periodically throughout the year, have them make drawings of the tree in their diaries to serve as a visual record of change. You may also wish to have children tape samples of leaves in their diaries.

April 7
It is spring. New, green leaves are covering the branches now.

Summer Fireworks

Children will enjoy painting a fireworks display to remind themselves of seasonal firework shows they have attended or have seen on television. Tell them to drop thick red, white, and blue blobs of tempera on construction paper. Then, using a toothpick, have them spread the blobs of paint outward in all directions.

Sing a Song of Summer

Sing songs that are reminiscent of summer. Possibilities include "Down by the Bay," "She Waded in the Water," "We All Scream for Ice Cream," and "Row, Row, Row Your Boat."

Sip a Summer Drink

Invite children to squeeze fresh lemons into glasses of iced water to make lemonade. Have them taste the refreshing drink first without and then with sugar.

Summer at the Seashore

Help children to make a collection of seashells. In a shallow box or on a tray, have children sort the shells by size, shape, and color. Then have them label the shells.

Autumn Is Here!

In areas where trees shed their leaves in the fall, let children rake leaves into a pile on the playground. Then encourage them to run and jump in the leaves. Have them notice the crunching, crackling sound the leaves make.

Autumn Harvest

Let children pick, wash, and taste samples of uncooked autumn foods such as pumpkin, apples, corn, cranberries, squash, and nuts.

Winter Fun

In those areas that experience snowfalls, have children toss and catch snowballs. If real snowballs are not available, use "snowballs" made of plastic, sponge, or Styrofoam.

Whipped Soap Painting

Invite children to make snow paintings. To make the "snow," mix 1 cup (250 ml) Ivory Snow powder with 1/2 cup (125 ml) warm water and whip with an eggbeater or wire whisk. When the mixture is frothy, invite children to dip a wooden craft stick into the "snow" and rub on dark construction paper.

Winter Wonders

Take a pan of water outside on a freezing cold day. Several hours later, bring the pan inside and have children observe and discuss the change. In areas that don't experience weather that is freezing cold, have children talk about what happens to water when it is put into the freezer section of the refrigerator. If possible, bring in ice cubes and set them on a table. Have children observe what happens to the ice.

Spring Blossoms

Children will enjoy painting spring trees. To make the tree trunk, have children place a blob of brown tempera on thick paper and blow on it with a straw. To make the blossoms, have children dip cotton-tipped swabs in pastel-color paint and then dab the swabs on the branches of the tree.

Signs of Spring

Bring to class one tree branch. Let children use a magnifying glass to examine the branch. Tell them to look for buds, blossoms, insects, and the like.

Spring Sights

After a spring shower, take children outside to look for rainbows. Or have them make their own rainbows. Demonstrate by having a volunteer stand with his or her back to the sun. Tell the volunteer to hold a garden hose so that the sunlight shines through the spray. Have the class look for the colors of the rainbow.

Books About Seasons

Lead a discussion of what happens to plants, animals, people, and the earth when the seasons change. Children will enjoy finding out about the changes as they read the following books:

- *Changing Seasons* by Rose Greydanus (Troll, 1983)
- *Fall* by Ann Blades (Lothrop, Lee, and Shepard, 1990)
- *January Brings the Snow: A Seasonal Hide and Seek Book* by Sara Coleridge (Orchard Books, 1989)
- *Kids and Seasons* by Kathy Darling (Monday Morning Books, 1989)
- *Muppet Babies Seasons* by Bonnie Worth (Macmillan, 1989)
- *Our House on the Hill* by Philippe Dupasquier (Penguin, 1990)

Using the Leaf Pattern

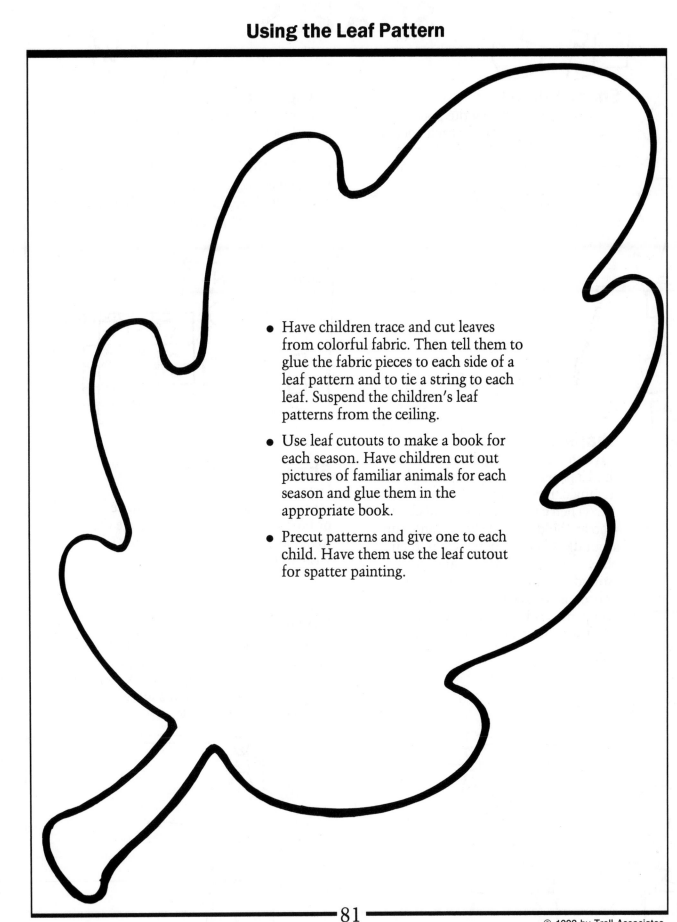

- Have children trace and cut leaves from colorful fabric. Then tell them to glue the fabric pieces to each side of a leaf pattern and to tie a string to each leaf. Suspend the children's leaf patterns from the ceiling.

- Use leaf cutouts to make a book for each season. Have children cut out pictures of familiar animals for each season and glue them in the appropriate book.

- Precut patterns and give one to each child. Have them use the leaf cutout for spatter painting.

SHAPES

Shape Poems

Encourage children to write poems about shapes. Tell them to write each poem in the shape of a circle, square, triangle, or rectangle. A "circle" poem is shown.

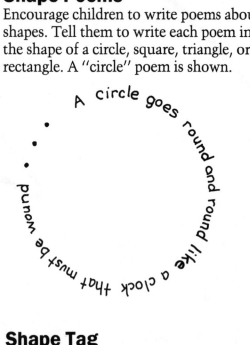

A circle goes round and round like a clock that must be round

Shape Tag

Have children sit in a circle. Give each child a paper circle, square, triangle, or rectangle. First, choose one child to be "It." Then call out a shape. All children who are holding that shape stand, run around the circle, and return to their place. "It," on the other hand, runs around the circle and tries to fill an unoccupied place before the previous occupant gets back. The player who is left without a place becomes the next "It."

Shape Hunt

Divide the class into small groups and assign each group a shape: circle, square, triangle, or rectangle. Have the members of each group look around the room to find and collect objects that have their assigned shape. Have children show their findings in a bar graph.

Shape Creatures

Have children arrange and glue geometric shapes together to create real or imaginary creatures. Encourage them to name their creatures and either to write or dictate stories about them.

Shape Pull

Divide the class into groups of four and give each group a rope. Challenge the members of each group to work together, using the rope, to form a square, a triangle, and a rectangle.

Holding Its Shape

Place different-shaped containers on a table. Have children pour water from one container into another. Point out that water takes on the shape of the container in which it is held. Have children name other things that take on the shape of their containers.

Shapes into Masterpieces

Borrow from the local library copies of cubist paintings by Pablo Picasso to show children. Point out the basic shapes the artist used. Then let children paint their own masterpieces. Remind them to use basic shapes the way Picasso did. Encourage children to sign their paintings and to give them titles. Display the children's paintings for all to enjoy.

Circle Collage

Collect or have children collect objects such as bottle caps, jar lids, buttons, and pie tins. Have children glue the objects to a paper plate to create a circle collage.

Shapes in the Sky

On a cloudy day, read *It Looked Like Spilt Milk* by Charles G. Shaw to children and talk about the shapes the characters saw in the clouds. Then take children outside. Have them look up at the sky and see if they can find clouds that are shaped like a triangle, a square, a rectangle, and a circle. Follow up by having children glue cotton on construction paper to create their own cloud shapes.

The Shape of Music

Show children how to play a triangle. Let interested children play the triangle as they sing a favorite song. Display instruments shaped like a circle (tambourine, cymbal, drum) and like a rectangle (piano, xylophone). Give children a chance to play each instrument and to name its shape.

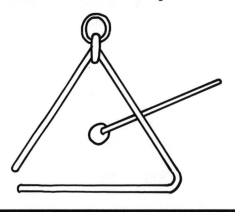

Square Dances

Teach the children a simple square dance. Help children form a square and play square dance music. Have opposing sides of the square perform movements in rhythm with the music. For example, those on sides 1 and 3 skip toward each other, clap hands, and walk back. Then sides 2 and 4 do the same. Additional movements such as bowing, tapping, swinging partners, shaking hands, and the like can be added as desired.

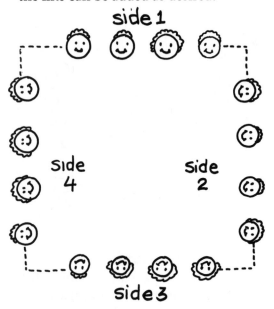

Share a Shape

Share the following books about shapes:
- *It Looked Like Spilt Milk* by Charles G. Shaw (Harper, 1988)
- *My First Look at Shapes* by Stephen Oliver (David McKay, 1990)
- *Playground Fun* by Sharon Gordon (Troll, 1988)
- *Shapes* by David Moss (Outlet, 1989)
- *Shapes* by Jan Pienkowski (Simon and Shuster, 1989)
- *Shapes* by Fiona Pragoff (Doubleday, 1989)
- *Shapes, Shapes, Shapes* by Tana Hoban (Greenwillow, 1986)

Sample a Shape

Provide prepared sugar cookie dough. Let children roll out the dough on wax paper and then use cookie cutters to cut the dough into squares, circles, triangles, and rectangles. Decorate, bake, and eat!

Fold a Shape

Help children fold their napkins into different shapes. Have them make a large square, a small square, a triangle, and a rectangle.

Using the Shape Patterns

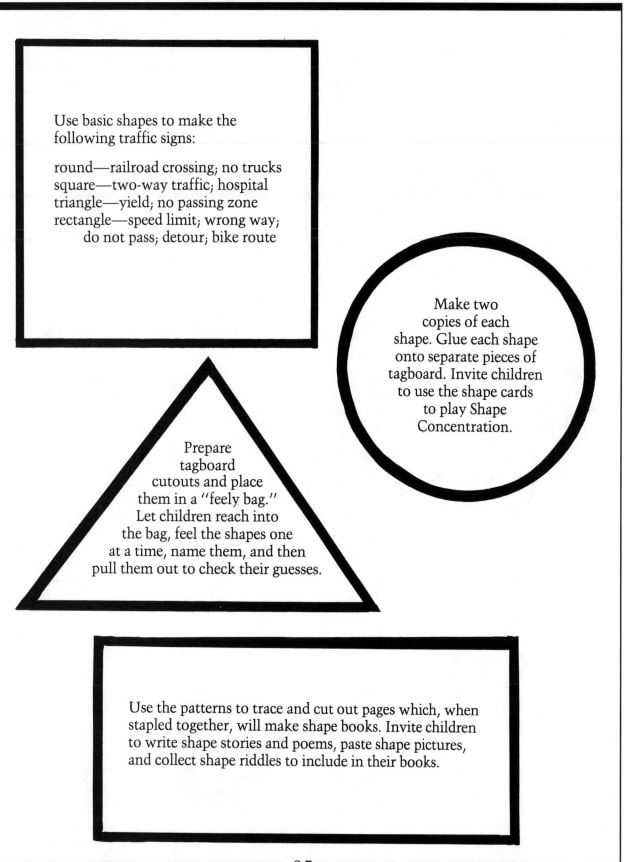

Use basic shapes to make the following traffic signs:

round—railroad crossing; no trucks
square—two-way traffic; hospital
triangle—yield; no passing zone
rectangle—speed limit; wrong way;
    do not pass; detour; bike route

Make two copies of each shape. Glue each shape onto separate pieces of tagboard. Invite children to use the shape cards to play Shape Concentration.

Prepare tagboard cutouts and place them in a "feely bag." Let children reach into the bag, feel the shapes one at a time, name them, and then pull them out to check their guesses.

Use the patterns to trace and cut out pages which, when stapled together, will make shape books. Invite children to write shape stories and poems, paste shape pictures, and collect shape riddles to include in their books.

SPACE

Star Finger Play

Demonstrate the actions as you say the finger play. Then invite children to join you as you say it again.

Twinkle, Twinkle, Little Star

Twinkle, twinkle, little star
(Open and close fingers above head.)

How I wonder what you are.
(Shrug shoulders, open hands.)

Up above the world so high
(Point to sky.)

Like a diamond in the sky.
(Use pointers and thumbs to make a diamond.)

Twinkle, twinkle, little star
(Open and close fingers above head.)

How I wonder what you are.
(Rest chin on closed hands.)

Planet Puzzle

Together with the class, list the names of the nine planets. Let children make crossword puzzles or search-a-word puzzles using the names. Copy and distribute the puzzles.

Sing a Song About Planets

Sing to the tune of "Mulberry Bush."

The Planet Song

Mercury, Venus, Earth, and Mars,
Mercury, Venus, Earth, and Mars,
Mercury, Venus, Earth, and Mars,
They all go round the Sun.
Jupiter and Saturn bright,
Uranus, Neptune, Pluto, too,
The planets nine go round the Sun
In our solar system.

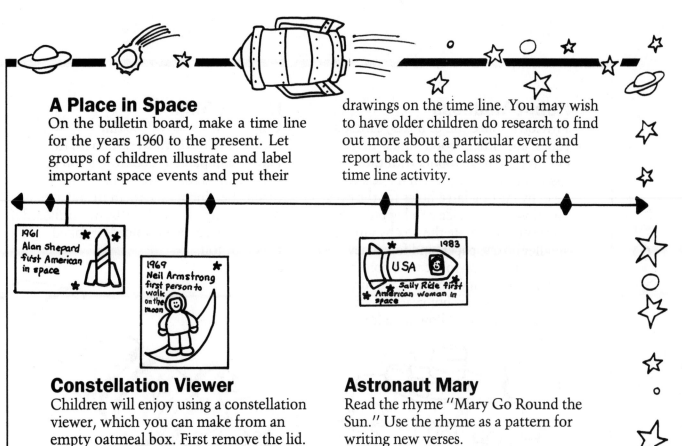

A Place in Space

On the bulletin board, make a time line for the years 1960 to the present. Let groups of children illustrate and label important space events and put their drawings on the time line. You may wish to have older children do research to find out more about a particular event and report back to the class as part of the time line activity.

1961 Alan Shepard first American in space

1969 Neil Armstrong first person to walk on the moon

1983 USA Sally Ride first American woman in space

Constellation Viewer

Children will enjoy using a constellation viewer, which you can make from an empty oatmeal box. First remove the lid. Then paint the inside of the box black. Next, use a pencil to poke a viewing hole in the bottom of the box.

Copy the pattern for the Little Dipper on the lid of the box. Use a thumbtack to punch out the stars in the constellation. Place the lid on the box. Invite children to hold the viewer up to the light and to describe what they see. You may wish to help children make their own viewers with other constellation patterns.

Astronaut Mary

Read the rhyme "Mary Go Round the Sun." Use the rhyme as a pattern for writing new verses.

Mary Go Round the Sun

Mary go round the sun,

Mary go round the moon,

Mary go round the chimney pots

On a Sunday afternoon.

Mary go round _____,

Mary go round _____,

Mary go round the _____

On a Sunday afternoon.

Robot Madness

Provide a collection of boxes, cardboard tubes, and other "good junk." Invite children to make robots with the materials. First help them make a robot head by cutting large holes for the eyes and nose on one side of a big box. Then have them decorate the box by gluing smaller boxes, paper, and foil. They may wish to paint the robot with poster paint or tempera. Children will have fun as they wear the robot gear and try to act like robots. Allow time for dramatic play.

Rocket Ship

Children will enjoy "blasting off" with a rocket ship made from cardboard tubes. Have them paint a tube from a roll of paper towels for the body of their rocket or shuttle. Encourage them to add details by attaching shorter lengths of cardboard tubes, fringed paper, folded or rolled paper, or foil.

Splash of Sun

Tell children to drop a small puddle of yellow paint onto a piece of paper. Then have them put a drop or two of orange and/or red paint in the center of the puddle. Invite children to use a toothpick to spread the colors outward to the edges of the paper.

Space Specials

Tell children to strap themselves in and get ready for a ride through space as you share with them these high-flying stories.

- *Does the Moon Change Shape?* by Meish Goldish (Raintree, 1989)
- *How the Moon Got in the Sky* by Addison-Wesley Staff (Addison-Wesley, 1989)
- *The Little Space Guy* by G. Kryptic Rodgers (Cyril Hayes, 1989)
- *The Moon* by Judith Greenberg and Helen Carey (Raintree, 1990)
- *Nora's Stars* by Satomi Ichikawa (Putnam, 1989)
- *Stars* by Roy Wandelmaier (Troll, 1985)
- *Tiny Star* (Macmillan, 1989)

Using the Spaceship Pattern

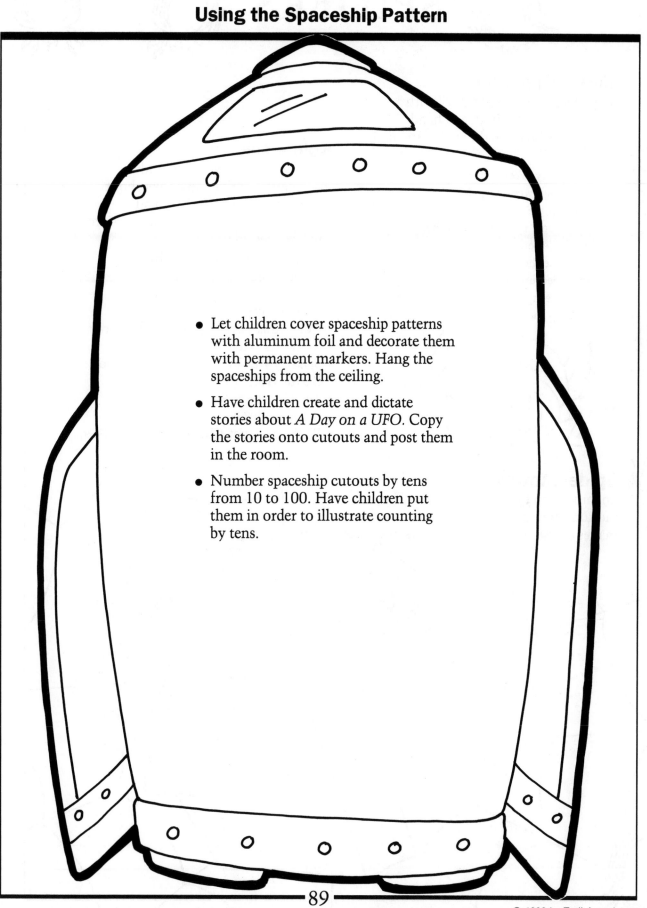

- Let children cover spaceship patterns with aluminum foil and decorate them with permanent markers. Hang the spaceships from the ceiling.

- Have children create and dictate stories about *A Day on a UFO*. Copy the stories onto cutouts and post them in the room.

- Number spaceship cutouts by tens from 10 to 100. Have children put them in order to illustrate counting by tens.

SPIDERS

Sing a Spider Song

Sing "Eensy, Weensy Spider" with children. Invite them to add hand motions to illustrate the spider, the rain, and the sun.

Eensy, Weensy Spider

The eensy, weensy spider
Went up the waterspout.
Down came the rain and washed
The spider out.
Out came the sun
And dried up all the rain.
So the eensy, weensy spider
Went up the spout again.

Spider Motions

Encourage children to pantomime the motions of a spider as it climbs on a web, makes a nest, and catches and eats insects.

Spin a Tale

Spin a web of imagination and information with good books about spiders. Include both fiction and nonfiction in your collection. Here are some suggested titles:

- *Amazing World of Spiders* by Janet Craig (Troll, 1990)
- *Charlotte's Web* by E.B. White (Harper, 1952)
- *I Can Read About Spiders* by Deborah Merrians (Troll, 1977)
- *Spider's Web* by Christine Back and Barrie Watts (Silver Burdett, 1986)
- *The Very Busy Spider* by Eric Carle (Putnam, 1989)
- *Wolfie* by Janet Chenery (Harper, 1969)

Spider's Play

Sing the song for the children. Then have children form a circle. Choose one child to be the "spider" and have him or her stand in the center of the circle. Have children sing the song together. As they sing, have the "spider" invite another child to join him or her in the "web." On the next verse, have children sing "two little spiders . . ." and invite another child to join them. Continue in this way until all children are in the "web."

A Spider Went out to Play

One little spider went out to play,
On a spider's web one day.
He had such enormous fun,
He asked another little spider to come.

Spiders' Webs

Explain to children that spiders spin their webs with thin threads of silk that they make inside their bodies. Tell them that the purpose of a spider's web is to catch insects for food. Children will be interested to know that different spiders spin different kinds of webs. Have children look for these types of webs in their environment:

orb web   *triangle web*

tangled web   *funnel web*

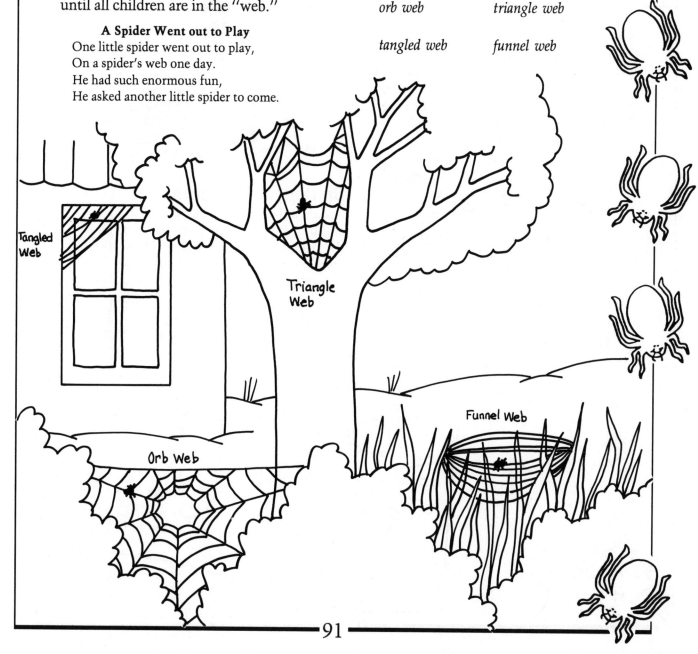

Tangled Web

Triangle Web

Orb Web

Funnel Web

Scope a Spider

Collect several different kinds of spiders, including the small garden spider or house spider and at least one large spider, such as a daddy longlegs. Invite children to look at each spider under a magnifying glass. Have them tell how many legs (eight) and body parts (two) a spider has. Have children look for other interesting characteristics that spiders have, such as fangs and spinnerette holes.

Spin a Web

Cut 8-inch (20-cm) frames from poster board. Punch holes at 1 inch (2.5 cm) intervals around the frame. Help children "thread" yarn through a bobby pin, then weave a web by sewing in and out of the holes going from top to bottom and side to side across the frame.

Spider Cups

Help children make friendly spiders. Use one cup from a Styrofoam egg carton. Poke pipe cleaners through the sides of the cup to make the spider's legs. Bend the ends of the pipe cleaners to make feet. Add eyes and fangs. Poke a pipe cleaner through the top of the cup to hang the spider from a door, bookshelf, or desk.

Spiders and Insects

Read Janet Chenery's book *Wolfie* to children. Then ask them to use facts in the story to help them write, tell, or draw diagrams that illustrate at least two differences between spiders and insects.

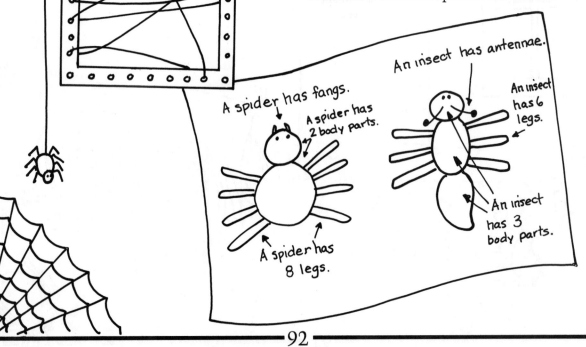

A spider has fangs.
A spider has 2 body parts.
A spider has 8 legs.

An insect has antennae.
An insect has 6 legs.
An insect has 3 body parts.

Using the Spider Pattern

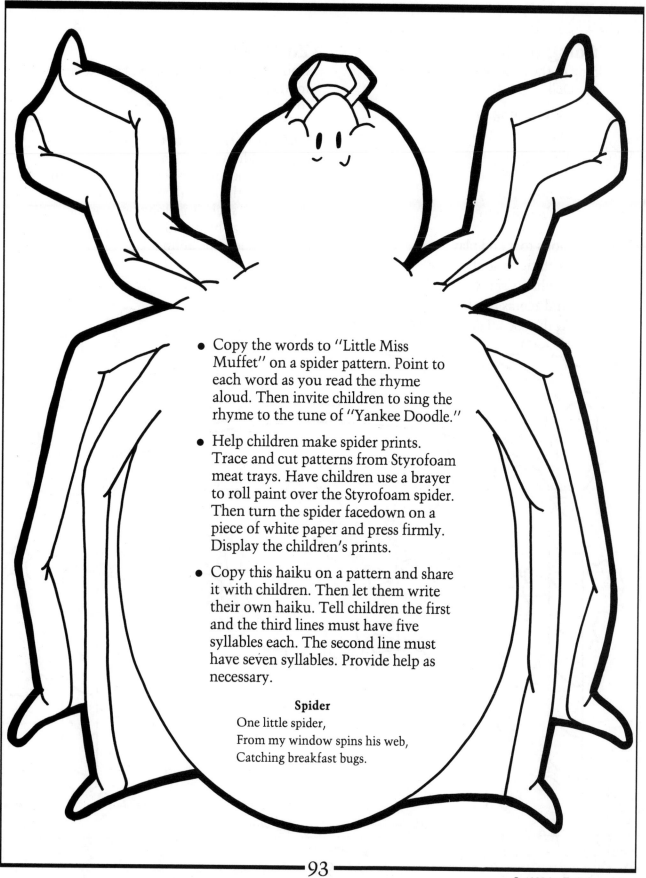

- Copy the words to "Little Miss Muffet" on a spider pattern. Point to each word as you read the rhyme aloud. Then invite children to sing the rhyme to the tune of "Yankee Doodle."

- Help children make spider prints. Trace and cut patterns from Styrofoam meat trays. Have children use a brayer to roll paint over the Styrofoam spider. Then turn the spider facedown on a piece of white paper and press firmly. Display the children's prints.

- Copy this haiku on a pattern and share it with children. Then let them write their own haiku. Tell children the first and the third lines must have five syllables each. The second line must have seven syllables. Provide help as necessary.

Spider
One little spider,
From my window spins his web,
Catching breakfast bugs.

ZOOS

Going to the Zoo

Sing to the tune of "The Farmer in the Dell."

We're Going to the Zoo

We're going to the zoo.
We'll see a kangaroo
And a cockatoo.
So how 'bout you?
We're going to the zoo.

Lions roar and play,
With tigers so they say.
Elephants spray
And zebras neigh
At the zoo all day.

Zoo Babies

Collect pictures of zoo babies and their mothers. Have children match each baby to the appropriate mother.

Guess Who at the Zoo

Have children take turns pantomiming different zoo animals. Encourage them to emphasize the special characteristics of the animal, such as its long neck or the way it swings by its tail. Let the other children guess the animal.

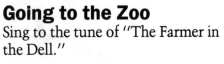

Model Zoo

Invite children to make a model of a zoo. Have them use clay to mold the animals. Help them to make individual living areas with cardboard boxes, Easter grass or hay, rocks, and water-filled pie tins. Encourage children to create "natural" settings for the animals. Different settings might be separated by moats or fences rather than by cages.

Zoo Socks

Use discarded socks to create various zoo animal puppets. Help children cut horns, ears, eyes, and spots from colorful construction paper. Staple, glue, or tape them to the socks. For the elephant's trunk, roll the foot of the sock to form the trunk. Use strips of tape to hold the trunk together. Invite children to play in small groups to create a brief skit for their puppets.

Zoo Menu

Invite a zookeeper to talk to the class about what zoo animals eat and how often they are fed. Then ask children to write a menu for lunch for an animal of their choice.

Encourage interested children to invent recipes for foods such as Zoo Stew, Elephant Porridge, or Alligator Surprise. Ask children to write directions for making the new recipes and to share their directions with the class. You might want to collect the recipes to make a cookbook entitled *Zoo Food, Anyone!* for everyone to share.

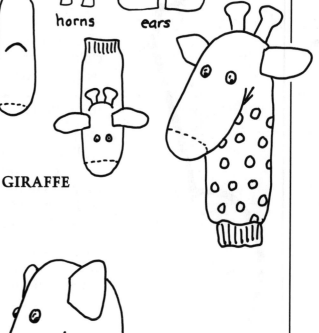

horns   ears

GIRAFFE

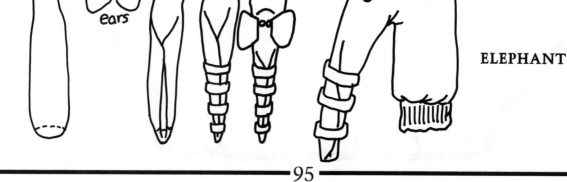

ears

ELEPHANT

Using the Lion Pattern

- Cut out and distribute patterns to children. Provide spotted and striped wallpaper. Let children use the patterns to trace and cut lions from the wallpaper.

- On lion cutouts, have children write riddles about zoo animals. Tell them to write the answers to their riddles on the backs of the cutouts. Staple the riddles together and add a lion cover to make a book entitled *Zoo Riddles*.

- Help children to find out what zoo doctors do. Prepare and distribute lion cutouts on which children can write and illustrate the duties of a zoo doctor.